crisis ready.

MELISSA AGNES

www.mascotbooks.com

Crisis Ready

For more information, please contact:
Mascot Books
620 Herndon Parkway #320
Herndon, VA 20170
info@mascotbooks.com

Library of Congress Control Number: 2018930359

CPSIA Code: PRBVG0218A
ISBN-13: 978-1-68401-413-2

Printed in the United States

LOVE FOR *crisis ready.*

Crisis Ready is a compelling reminder that managing a crisis is not the same as managing a company. If you think the same management techniques that allow you to win at business will enable you to weather a crisis, you are doomed.

In a crisis, emotions run high, people revert to habits instead of the plan, information travels quickly—whether it is accurate or not—and the effects of your decisions can be long-lived. Don't allow the crisis management plan sitting on your shelf to give you a false sense of confidence. Read this book and then get to work at making crisis management muscle memory for your organization.

David Struhs, *Vice President, Domtar, Corporate Services and Sustainability*

Melissa Agnes *gets it!* Preparedness—*or being ready*—is the key to crisis management. In business, as in life, a crisis never gives us advance notice of when and where it will show up. And, since it doesn't care about the slick organizational charts of most companies, it doesn't give us the courtesy of limiting its strike to only one of those cute little square boxes—its ripple effects can reach far into the deep corners of the entire organization. Agnes teaches us that the key to dealing with a crisis is to anticipate all the places it can strike, and *then go there* and lie in wait with a plan. At McDonald's Corporation, where I was the General Counsel, we constantly played the "what if" game: "What if" a child is injured in one of our Playlands? "What if" our stock price has a sudden drop? "What if" the computer system breaks down? "What if" an environmentalist criticizes our packaging, or a nutritionist criticizes our food? The "what if" game paid dividends by giving us the head start that Melissa Agnes urges—*be there and be ready!* Shame on you if you are surprised by a crisis.

Shelby Yastrow, *Retired General Counsel, Executive Vice President and Secretary of McDonald's*

Intelligent. Intuitive. Unabashedly gutsy. Melissa Agnes dismantles crisis clichés, shakes you awake, and takes you on a compelling and insightful journey that will ensure your organization is crisis ready.

Scot Wheeler, *Retired Global Director of Issues Management and Crisis Communications, The Dow Chemical Company*

Every business of any size needs to read *Crisis Ready*. Melissa Agnes demonstrates why she is a leading authority on timely, intelligent, and appropriate communications in moments of crisis. If United Airlines had read this book in 2009, my *United Breaks Guitars* YouTube video would never have happened. I'm almost glad she hadn't written it yet.

Dave Carroll, *Singer-songwriter, speaker, and creator of* United Breaks Guitars

Speaking as a communications professional, there is no one better at crisis communications than Melissa Agnes. She has a calm and patient way of looking at the entire picture, assessing the challenge, and providing recommendations that work in less time than it takes you to say "crisis communications." As social media came into the fold, she was one of the first—and most trustworthy— professionals to explain the differences between a crisis, an issue, and a quick social media event. She goes into each of these in-depth in *Crisis Ready*, while also providing a smart roadmap to help you build your reputation so when there is a crisis, you're prepared. With case studies, homework, rules, and tests, you will find yourself ready to handle anything by the end of the book. Read it, absorb it, take lots of notes, and create your crisis preparedness program.

Gini Dietrich, *CEO of Arment Dietrich, founder and author of* Spin Sucks

The speed of a crisis in the digital age can quickly overwhelm organizations ill-prepared with outdated strategies centered around press releases and bureaucratic layers of approvals for communication. *Crisis Ready* serves as a strategic blueprint to help organizations prepare for and successfully navigate turmoil, all while building trust and confidence with their stakeholders.

Captain Chris Hsiung, *Law Enforcement Executive*

The ultimate guide to doing things right before it all goes wrong. Every businessperson should have a copy of *Crisis Ready* on their desk.

Jay Baer, *Founder of Convince & Convert, author of* Hug Your Haters

Contents

INTRO

ARE YOU
CRISIS READY?

It's Tuesday night, past 9:30 pm, and you're enjoying a relaxing evening with your family. Suddenly, your phone lights up with a Google Alert. *That's strange*, you think. Normally Tuesday evenings are quiet. You check to see what's going on...

Death Toll Rises In TrainCompany Train Derailment.

Your heart instantly sinks to the pit of your stomach. As a member of the executive team at *TrainCompany*, you know this is going to be bad.

You instinctively turn your television to your go-to news station and start scanning news coverage online. You're met with horrifying pictures, videos of emergency responders, and livestream footage being taken by passersby. The hashtag #TrainCompanyCrash is starting to trend on social media, and you quickly realize that the story has already gone national.

The headlines keep coming...

TrainCompany Terrifying Wreck Captured On Live Video

Catastrophic TrainCompany Derailment Will Significantly Disrupt Service

TrainCompany Deadly Crash: Economic Impact To Be Disastrous

You notice that people are already asking questions and making assumptions. Meanwhile, you have a ton of questions of your own. *How did this happen? Was it negligence or a freak accident? How many people are injured? What will the death toll be? Who's onsite? Why have I not been notified? Does anybody else know? How long will operations be down? Who's monitoring social media and the news media? How will we respond? What's the impact going to be? How will we control this?*

You take a deep breath and call the other members of your executive team.

If you were to find your organization faced with a devastating, and viral situation next Tuesday evening, what would you do? Would your team know who to summon and how to convene? Would you be able to gather the necessary facts? How long *would* that process take? Do you feel confident that your team would know exactly how to respond in a way that would enable the organization to position itself as the credible leader of the situation? What's the protocol for this type of high-impact scenario within your organization? Would you be crisis ready?

I've been an entrepreneur my entire adult life. After starting a small web development company in 2009 with my then-partner, Colt, geared towards helping companies develop their web presence and digital branding strategies, I became interested in crisis management by a fateful fluke one afternoon in 2010.

I had been catching up on some reading. If you can remember, a decade ago everyone was excited about the benefits of social media, mobile technology, the real-time news cycle, and the opportunities that these fast-paced tools offered to brands. However, it struck me that afternoon that very few were assessing the *risks* of such tools. With this realization, a spark ignited inside me and I spent the next year voraciously reading anything I could get my hands on related to crisis management.

And it was a good thing I had, because as fate would have it, I was about to be thrown into the deep end.

One early morning, the VP of a real estate investment trust, one of our clients, called me in a panic.

> Melissa, our president is in the car with a prospective investor and the radio is reporting that one of our buildings is about to explode—which isn't true—and apparently, the story started on Twitter...what the hell is Twitter?! We're going to lose this investor. We need your help!"

You see, we had just launched this organization's website and were about to begin discussions about a social media strategy for their brand, so we were the first people that came to their minds when they learned that Twitter was an "online thing."

I hurried to my client's office and within roughly thirty minutes we had the media correcting themselves and had the company up and running on Twitter—but more importantly, we had Twitter streaming to their website's homepage as we knew their investors would be navigating to their website, not to Twitter, for news and updates concerning the incident.

To make a long story short, the next day I received a call from the president of the company thanking me. He said that not only had their unit price not gone down since the day before, but it had actually gone up a cent!

This confirmed my hunch, and I realized that we were onto something important. People needed these services and we had discovered a natural aptitude in providing them. With that, Colt and I decided to dive in and follow our instincts and passion. We finished the client projects we were working on, and soon began focusing on "crisis management for the 21st century" full time.

With a limited marketing budget, we couldn't take on expensive marketing tactics, so I utilized my digital branding experience and dedicated myself to blogging five days a week. It was through blogging that I began to get my concepts, thoughts, and strategies out into the world.

And it worked.

Right place, right time, right message. Before long, I had some brilliant long-standing crisis management professionals reaching out to me, saying,

> We don't know whether this whole social media thing is a fad or a trend, and we're nearing retirement so we don't necessarily want to learn it, but we definitely know that our clients need your services now. Can we partner?"

We were fortunate to gain incredible mentors who opened their client lists up to us and the rest, as they say, is history.

What made my blog unique at the time, and therefore made me stand out in the profession, is that I was addressing social media, real-time communication, and mobile technology differently from most. I was examining and exploring the challenges and risks, as well as the opportunities within those challenges and risks that were prevalent to every organization. Through this, I was boldly addressing the fact that the old ways of crisis management would no longer cut it, and that these risks now applied to every company and brand, not just the big names.

It used to be that organizations—the smart ones, anyway—would create a crisis management plan, store it on a shelf or in a file, and rest assured that if a crisis were to strike they would be ready, as they had a plan just waiting to be activated. Today, choosing to *rely* on a crisis management plan is no longer sufficient. In fact, it puts you at a disadvantage.

In this always-on digital era, crises unfold and escalate so quickly that by the time you reach for that plan, you risk already being behind, losing control of the narrative of the incident. The more you lose control, the harder it is to regain and the more trust, credibility, and goodwill you lose with your key stakeholders. This means that today's Crisis Response Penalty, or CRP, can be dire.

THE CRISIS RESPONSE PENALTY

The CRP is an equation I use to calculate the immediate monetary impact of a crisis on an organization, in association with the organization's crisis response. As you'll see throughout this book, there's often a link between the response strategy—whether it be timing and / or adequacy of the response—and the direct financial impact on the organization. A strong and timely response helps mitigate escalation of the incident and enables the organization to better own the crisis, whereas a delayed and inadequate response will do the exact opposite.

Additionally, there's also something I call the "soft CRP." When we evaluate the soft CRP of an organization's management of an issue or a crisis, we examine the reputational impact of the response, especially over the long-term. What I've learned and seen far too often is that short-term damage often leaves long-term scars, whether the organization is immediately aware of them or not.

The reality is that there is a lot of complexity and a lot at stake when things go wrong. Therefore, crisis management can no longer be about simply relying on a plan that sits on a shelf. Rather,

CRISIS READY RULE

If you don't own the crisis, the crisis will own you.

it needs to be about developing a culture in which people are taught and empowered to mitigate risk in real time, understand expectations, and make smart decisions quickly—a culture where crisis and issue management is an instinctive and reflexive team collaboration, rather than a linear (and often times, siloed) plan that is meant to be followed point by point.

However, this is not to say that a crisis plan is not an important part of your crisis preparedness and management. The act of creating a crisis management plan is an invaluable exercise that will go an extremely long way towards helping your organization prevent and manage crises and issues. Nevertheless, the fact remains that today a plan is but *one* piece of a much larger puzzle—a puzzle that involves implementing a crisis ready program, not just a plan, that is embedded into the very culture of your organization. It is by achieving this level of preparedness that you become truly crisis ready, and thus build an invincible brand.

In order to achieve this level of brand invincibility, there are five fundamental steps and processes to be undertaken. These five fundamentals are:

1. Conducting an audit of your organization's current mindset and culture. This will enable you to understand where you currently sit on the spectrum of crisis readiness, and identify the areas within your organization that will require some dedicated focus.

2. Seeking to fully understand the many variables and impacts that you will face, like it or not, in a real-time crisis. This is the educational component that will help the team gain realistic perspective on the true breadth and scope of crises. It will also help you gain the necessary buy-in and support required, as implementing a crisis ready culture needs to start from the top down.

3. Holding interviews and sparking discussions that will enable you to identify and understand your organization's high-risk scenarios and key stakeholder groups, providing you with the information required to develop comprehensive crisis management strategies.

4. Designing your program, which will consist of everything from your crisis management governance structure to your action plans and targeted crisis communication strategies.

5. Undergoing regular exercises that will enable you to implement the program, as well as train and empower your team to develop the skills required to be truly crisis ready.

CRISIS READY MODEL

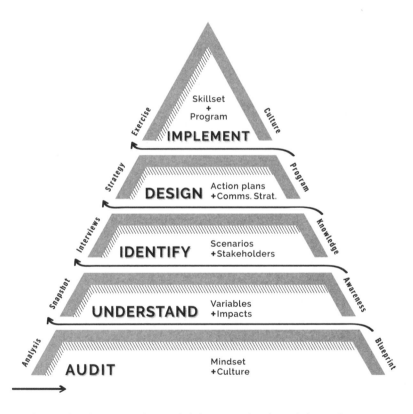

This is the Crisis Ready Model that I've developed throughout my years of helping organizations—which include everything from government entities, financial institutions, non-profits, healthcare organizations, energy companies, consumer goods organizations, technology companies, and more—implement crisis ready cultures, and manage real-world crises.

By undertaking this approach to your crisis preparedness, you too will be able to provide your team with the right tools, strategies, and skills to successfully manage any issue or crisis that may strike your organization. The purpose of this book is to take you on this journey, and share with you the exact processes that I employ with my clients. This model, the work that I do with my clients, and the programs that I deliver on stages around the world, continue to inspire and impassion me. Why? Because I've seen the results and benefits, time and time again, that they provide to organizations of all different types, industries, and sizes. I want you and your organization to reap the same advantages and flourish from the same benefits. I want to help you build an INVINCIBLE brand that will successfully weather any storm.

If your phone starts illuminating with gut-wrenching news, and you know that a viral issue or terrible crisis has struck your organization, I want you and your team to instinctively know exactly what to do to quickly get ahead of and de-escalate the situation. This was my objective in writing this book. This objective is what fueled the long nights and early mornings, the strategy sessions and, frankly, the excitement that went into the writing process.

You may have already noticed, upon picking up and quickly scrolling through these pages, that this is not your typical (boring) crisis management book. Crises and crisis management techniques have changed and evolved over the last several years, and so should crisis management literature. In writing this book, I really wanted to create a helpful guide that would provide you with everything you need to implement a crisis ready culture and be fully prepared to manage any type of issue or crisis that may come your way—but in a way that is fun and interesting. I hope you'll find that I have accomplished this, and I'd love to hear your thoughts, comments, and questions along the way.

Though don't be fooled! I'm not saying it will be easy. Implementing a crisis ready culture, and thus building an invincible brand, will involve a lot of hard work, but if you decide to travel down this road with me, you will find the rewards well worth your time and effort.

PUTTING THIS BOOK TO WORK FOR YOU

As becoming crisis ready requires a deep-rooted cultural component, it was important that this book be designed for every member of your team. However, not every chapter will apply to every team member, so here is how I propose reading this book:

- Leadership and decision makers will benefit from reading the book in its entirety.

- Those tasked with creating your crisis ready program should read the book twice: once to fully grasp the full context and scope of the process, and the second time to dive in and begin creating and implementing the program.

- All employees will benefit from reading chapters one through five, and chapter ten.

No matter the type or size of your organization, choosing to take this path and build an INVINCIBLE brand will serve your company on so many levels, and I'm so excited to be taking this journey with you!

Are you ready? If so, I'll meet you over in chapter one!

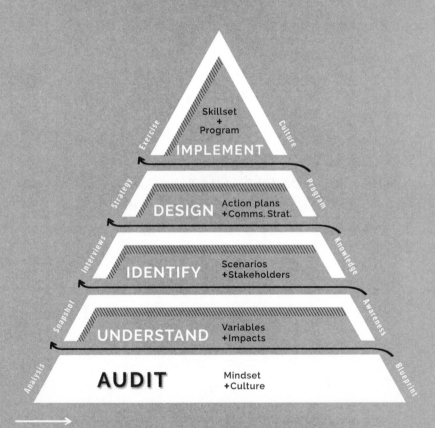

01

YOUR THOUGHTS AROUND CRISIS

Effective crisis preparedness begins with the right mindset, and a willingness and commitment to change the areas of your business that do not coincide with this mindset. But what's the right mindset? Let me give you an example. A LinkedIn connection of mine once wrote the following as a comment on one of my articles:

Why CRISIS is a bad word:
People—

C Create their problems;

R React by blaming others;

I Infer that all will be okay;

S Secure themselves behind false claims;

I Independent they become instead of working as a collective; and

S Sue to protect the little honor they have left.

My LinkedIn connection is correct—if this is an organization's mindset and approach to crisis management, then crisis should indeed be a bad word. In fact, it should be synonymous with "failure" because if this is your approach to crisis management, you're doomed! Needless to say, this is a clear example of the wrong mindset.

I'm a firm believer in the idea that your outlook and your energy shape your results and, ultimately, your life. And while I'm not going to get all philosophical on you, I do bring this approach to every aspect of my crisis management and preparedness work with clients, whether I'm consulting or on stage presenting a keynote—and so should you. The way you choose to look at, prepare for, and empower your teams to see and respond to negative situations directly shapes the outcome of those negative situations. When I see a crisis, my first thoughts are:

C COMMUNICATE

R RESPECT

I INITIATE

S SHOW

I ISSUE-MANAGE

S SUSTAIN

C IS FOR "COMMUNICATE"

As we'll see a little later on, you can do everything right behind the scenes, but if you don't communicate in a timely, transparent, and compassionate manner, all these behind the scenes efforts will be for nothing. However, as you may know, communication can be difficult. It can be hard to communicate quickly when you don't have all the facts, and it can be difficult to get legal and other departments and executives on board with timely and transparent communications. However, these difficulties don't negate the fact that effective communication is essential for successful crisis management.

R IS FOR "RESPECT"

As we'll see later, emotions run high in times of crisis and emotion is one of the key factors that can quickly send a crisis going viral against your organization. It's also important to remember that logic can never trump emotion. So, to have your story heard and resonate with your stakeholders on an emotional level, you need to be ready and willing to first respect and validate their feelings and their sentiment towards the incident and the organization.

I IS FOR "INVESTIGATE"

What happened? How did it happen? Why did it happen? In order to get to the root cause of an incident, you will need to investigate. Depending on the scenario, your team, your board, and / or third party experts may need to conduct this investigation. Having the right mindset means that, in a crisis, you will care about uncovering the root cause of the incident—because without the answers as to how and why the crisis happened in the first place, how can you ever aim to fix the problem and improve?

S IS FOR "SHOW"

To position your organization as the voice of trust, credibility, and leadership in a crisis, you must show strong, emotionally intelligent leadership that prioritizes people above processes and bottom lines. Demonstrate and prove this in *all* aspects of your crisis management, including your choice actions, not just your choice words.

I IS FOR "ISSUE-MANAGE"

One of the secrets of crisis prevention is effective issue management. This means your organization needs to prioritize issue management by empowering team members to proactively detect issues in real time, and then to take corrective actions to mitigate their escalation.

S IS FOR "SUSTAIN"

Sustain your business and your brand's reputation by choosing to learn from mistakes and by committing to improvement and positive evolution. This means implementing corrective actions and behaviors to right wrongs and ensure certain incidents never happen again. You won't be forgiven for making the same mistake twice, so don't.

Do you see how this way of thinking turned "crisis" from a bad word into a more positive one? The mindset in which you approach crises and their management changes everything. It is the differentiating factor between burying your head in the sand or taking the wrong approach to crisis management, and turning negative situations into opportunities that will connect you more closely with your stakeholders and make you a good example for others to learn from.

PRACTICING AN OPPORTUNITY-SEEKING MINDSET

The way you look at the world is your choice; the way you react to circumstances is your choice; and the culture you embed within your organization is your choice. This is a very powerful choice indeed. It can enable you to embrace today's new realities, by choosing to see the opportunities amidst the chaos. Choosing to have and implement this mindset can change your company from the ground up, making it a better place to *be* and ultimately, making it truly crisis-resilient.

Now, I realize that this choice is easier said than implemented for many organizations. It can be quite overwhelming to watch your brand be associated with a negative incident—especially if the incident is garnering lots of unwanted attention. Adding to the complexity, in times of crisis human beings tend to revert to practices that they are familiar and comfortable with. This means that until your company practices and hones the right mindset to the point where it is an instinctive reflex, it will be easy to revert to your current culture—whatever that may be—when times get tough.

So, let's practice this mindset in theory, before we take it to reality. Feel free to bring examples like the one you're about to read to your team to help them embed the right mindset and instinctive approach to issues and crises as well (FYI, I go into much further detail about bringing these types of exercises to your team in chapter nine).

What Would
You Do?

Recently, a municipality I work with called me to say that they had launched a hashtag campaign to promote their city and that it had taken a turn for the worse. Their big question was "Oh, no! What should we do?"

This hashtag campaign took place on Twitter and used the hashtag #citystories, where "city" was the actual city's name. Using this hashtag, my client asked their community to weigh in on what made their city great. The goal was to provoke conversation and to ultimately inspire outsiders to choose to vacation in their lovely city in the future. The problem was, while many of the tweets were positive about the city, many of them were not. And when I say "many," I'm talking about hundreds in a short amount of time, all publicly airing community members' complaints and grievances for the world—and future tourists—to read about.

When my client called, asking me what they should do, the answer was instantly clear to me. But before I give you my answer, I want you to take a moment to think of yours.

What would you do if you found your company in this type of "campaign-gone-wrong" situation? Would you consider stopping the campaign if it wasn't developing into the purely positive one you were aiming for? Would you choose only to focus on the positive comments and tweets, ignoring the negative ones? If you had to face this type of attention-grabbing situation, what would your organization's natural inclination be? Be honest.

Now that you've put some thought into it, here's what my response to my client was: "What a phenomenal opportunity!" Do you see why? Or are you as flabbergasted as they were at my enthusiasm? Let me explain.

The city's goal was to start a dialogue with their community and to inspire outsiders to choose their city as their future vacation destination. The good news was that they had clearly attained engagement, which is often the hardest part. How they chose to respond to this engagement, both the negative and positive sides of it, would make all the difference in the ultimate success of the campaign and the relationships they share with their community.

Their community members obviously cared enough about their city to voice their grievances, which in and of itself is a positive thing. Now it was up to the city to choose to actively listen, engage, and turn this situation into an unexpected opportunity.

> In all honesty, this should not have been an unexpected situation. The truth is that, had the city been crisis ready, their processes and mindset would have enabled them to identify this as a potential risk while developing the campaign. Therefore, they would not have been caught off guard. They would have been ready to immediately turn the situation into an opportunity.

So, what was the opportunity? The opportunity was that they had a chance to gain a better understanding of their community members and their sentiment towards the city. By choosing:

* Communicating, remembering that communication is a two-way street;

- Respecting and validating the concerns of their community members;

- Investigating ways that the city can ameliorate;

- Showing true leadership;

- Empowering issue management (which is what this situation is: an issue, not a crisis—but more on that later); and ultimately

- Sustaining the city's reputation by committing to improvement and evolution. The city had an opportunity to fix some lingering issues, building a deeper sense of community and truly making their city one to be proud of and one worthy of visits and support from others.

Therefore, what may have first appeared as a negative turn of events was ultimately a blessing—a blessing that required the right mindset to spot and make the most of. Let's face it, many organizations would have only seen that the campaign didn't go as anticipated and would have shut it down before it got worse, not realizing how this conversation could build a stronger community and an even stronger city.

Conducting an audit of your culture and taking measures to adopt the right mindset is the first step in implementing your crisis ready culture, because the truth is that most negative incidents present positive opportunities if you choose to see them that way. Choosing to see the opportunities, rather than only seeing the challenges and obstacles, will help you make the right decisions in a crisis.

While much of the world is watching—and trust me, many will be scrutinizing your every move in a crisis or viral issue—is a great time to

CRISIS READY RULE

Never launch a new product, campaign, or communication without assessing the potential risk.

showcase your values, your caring, and your willingness to do the right thing, even when the right thing is sometimes the more difficult choice to make. Being able to do this effectively starts with having the right mindset and implementing a culture that matches it.

MAKE THIS MINDSET A PART OF YOUR CULTURE, AND ACHIEVE CRISIS-RESILIENCE

The best-managed crises are the ones no one ever hears about. That's because they were so well managed that they never escalated to the point where they captured unwanted attention. The proper mindset is the first skill that will help enable your team to intercept and mitigate crises before they happen.

While I do believe that negative events or situations have a silver lining, I disagree with the old adage that "any publicity is good publicity." Negative incidents chip away at the trust your stakeholders have in your organization and its credibility. Therefore, if you can avoid a negative incident, or prevent one from escalating further, you need to do so.

To successfully manage a crisis, you need to be quick enough to spot the problem and make the right decisions in the heat of the moment. Accomplishing this requires more than a plan. It requires a culture that spots opportunities, embraces proactivity, and cultivates valuable instincts.

It takes a culture that will enable your team to make the right decisions under scrutiny and tough circumstances—not because that's what your crisis ready program says to do, but because doing the right thing has always been rewarded in your organization, so it comes naturally.

Crisis-resilient culture: a real-world example

I love to use Zappos, the online shoe company, as an example of this type of crisis-resilient, emotionally intelligent culture. For starters, Zappos's goal is "to be the company that provides the absolute best service online—not just in shoes, but in any category."[1] Not a bad goal!

Their mission is about delivering happiness. This, as a mission, is extremely powerful. This means that every moment of every day, Zappos employees are encouraged and empowered to "deliver happiness" to their customers. This culture shapes the mindset of their employees, enabling them to continuously make smart decisions for the right reasons.

For example, Zappos has a free shipping return policy that allows you to return their shoes within fifteen days. However, in order to do this, you have to go to UPS yourself to ship them out. One customer, Zaz Lamarr, had ordered a bunch of shoes for her mom, some of which didn't fit, so she requested the return shipping label from Zappos and planned to return them. Sadly, her mom passed away before she got the chance. On her personal blog,[2] Lamarr described the following experience she had with the online shoe company, shortly after her mother's death:

"... I had an email from Zappos asking about the shoes, since they hadn't received them. I was just back and not ready to deal with that, so I replied that my mom had died but that I'd send the shoes as soon as I could. They emailed back that they had arranged with UPS to pick up the shoes, so I wouldn't have to take the time to do it myself. I was so touched. That's going against corporate policy.

Yesterday, when I came home from town, a florist delivery man was just leaving. It was a beautiful arrangement in a basket with white lilies and roses and carnations. Big and lush and fragrant. I opened the card, and it was from Zappos. I burst into tears. I'm a sucker for kindness, and if that isn't one of the nicest things I've ever had happen to me, I don't know what is. So...

IF YOU BUY SHOES ONLINE, GET THEM FROM ZAPPOS.

With hearts like theirs, you know they're good to do business with."

This, like many other Zappos stories, demonstrates how their mission to "deliver happiness" results in employees going above and beyond to create positive emotional experiences for their customers. This is obviously great for their day-to-day business, as it builds relationships based on core values and provides unforgettable experiences for their customers. But from a crisis readiness perspective, with this type of behavior and mindset encouraged and rewarded daily, can you imagine Zappos mismanaging a crisis? I certainly can't, not if they have this type of focus guiding their every decision!

In one of their company culture videos,[3] Vanessa Lawson, the Senior Trainer at Zappos, says,

> [When] you work here, you do become a better person just because of the core values, because of the culture, because of the directors and the leadership."

Saying that an organization's culture makes you a better human being is a tremendous statement. It's a testament to the mindset they've embedded and the choices leadership makes daily to lead by example.

Of course, when I mention Zappos as an example of this type of culture, people often argue, "Zappos is a relatively new company. It's easier to start off this way than it is to change a culture that has been siloed for decades."

Sure. It's difficult to change an existing culture and mindset. But I never said it was going to be easy. Nothing worth doing ever is. The reality is that times have changed and the organizations that want to be truly crisis ready need to be willing to adapt to these changes. I keep mentioning that this is a choice—and it is one that takes conscious effort and discipline.

Organizations that implement this mindset aren't afraid of trial and error. By embracing the need for this mindset, they consciously chose to take experimental steps in the right direction every day. At the start, their steps were small, enabling them to test what worked and what did not, without their errors being too drastic; yet the learning moments were always pillars of the process. So, don't be afraid to start small and certainly don't let the risk of errors halt you. Take one small step in the right direction every day. These steps will add up before you know it.

So, if you can see how powerful it would be to create a culture that focuses on relationship-building and spotting opportunities to create wonderful experiences for your stakeholders, then there are simple decisions you can choose to make every day which will help inspire the right mindset and cultivate instincts that will prove invaluable in a real-time crisis. One of these decisions is to choose to focus on trust.

A CRITICAL INGREDIENT FOR CRISIS READINESS

Stakeholder trust is something that every organization naturally strives to achieve. Having stakeholders who trust in the brand affects everything from reputation to business longevity. But an added value of trust-building that many don't necessarily think or know about is what trust can do for your crisis management.

Strong stakeholder trust earns your organization the benefit of the doubt at the onset of a crisis. This benefit of the doubt gives you unique crisis management advantages. For example, imagine that a horrific crisis strikes your organization and, in the initial moments of the news breaking, your key stakeholders' instinctive reaction is to say to themselves:

> There must be more to the story. I'm going to wait to hear what the organization has to say, before I make any judgements or rash decisions."

The power behind this benefit of the doubt is that stakeholders' hearts and minds are open to hearing your side of the story *first*, instead of instantly believing the potential rumors, speculation, and third party discussions that may already be taking place. Why? Because they trust the organization and the people behind it.

When I think of an organization that consciously works every day to build trust with its stakeholders, I always think of the Mountain View Police Department (MVPD) in Silicon Valley, California. The community of Mountain View has so much trust in their police department that whenever the media reports something negative about the community or the police department, the community's natural inclination is to say, "unless Mountain View PD posts it, we don't believe it."

Now *that* is powerful trust!

But this trust wasn't built overnight.

Law enforcement across North America has been experiencing an industry-wide crisis over the past several years, where trust between police agencies and their communities is at an all-time low. And yet, MVPD clearly does not have this problem. Why? Because they've worked hard and consciously to implement the right culture and mindset within their agency, and part of that culture and mindset means that they focus every single day on proactively building and strengthening the trust they share with their community.

How do they do this? Let's look at some examples. Knowing that their community is active on Twitter, among other places, MVPD began posting images like these with the following types of messages attached to it: "Psssst, hey Mountain View, we're 'hiding' on the corner of El Camino and Shoreline. Please slow down."

When they first started posting these types of messages, the community would tweet back with responses like, "Hey @MountainViewPD, how do you expect to catch us speeding if you tell us where you're hiding?!"

This seems like a reasonable response, doesn't it? It was MVPD's replies to these responses that changed everything. They would reply to these tweets with messages that explained that their goal *isn't* to catch people speeding. Their goal is road and community safety. So, if sharing where their officers are stationed makes people reflect and slow down, then they're achieving their goal.

These atypical communications fostered real trust. All of a sudden, the community started realizing that their law enforcement agency wasn't out to give them citations or meet quotas. Instead, they realized that MVPD truly cares about the people within the community and, as a result, real relationships started forming.

This is an example of an outward facing initiative, but MVPD doesn't just take external initiatives. For example, once they began to see the wonderful messages of gratitude and trust that were being shared with the police department on social media, Shino Tanaka, MVPD's public information officer who headed the department's social media initiatives at the time, wanted to make sure that their officers were feeling the love of their community as well.

You see, Shino knew that their officers were not necessarily online reading the messages on social media, because they were out in the field. They were on the streets, doing their jobs. This meant that while they were making the efforts to build trust, serve, and protect, they weren't able to read all the messages of gratitude that were being shared with them online. Shino decided to print these messages and tape them to the walls of the precinct. She brought the online community into a space where the officers would have the opportunity to see them. This simple gesture helped strengthen the bonds between the police officers and the community.

Captain Chris Hsiung of Mountain View Police Department words it beautifully. He says that every day, MVPD works to put deposits into their bank of community trust. In crises, they have to make withdrawals from that bank of community trust, but the goal is that when that inevitably happens, they have enough trust in the bank that it does not become overdrawn. When this theory was tested, MVPD's efforts and mindset proved to have been well worth the effort.

Learn more about the strategies MVPD implements to build community trust: melissaagnes.com/mvpdpodcast

In May of 2014, Mountain View Police Department experienced a serious internal crisis, when one of their law enforcement officers was arrested for child pornography. But because MVPD had the right mindset and had spent time building a strong relationship with their community, they instinctively knew what to do to get ahead of the story by taking the "CRISIS" approach that we saw earlier in this chapter:

They communicated quickly and transparently. MVPD didn't wait for the media to report on the arrest. They got ahead of the story by publishing an open letter[4] to their community, where they were forthright and honest, sincere and relatable.

They respected and validated the community's feelings. Sure, people were upset to hear of the news and they openly expressed this. But MVPD didn't shy away. They validated their community's feelings by answering each and every comment and message that was shared, and they conveyed their own devastation towards the incident. This helped make them human and relatable, bringing them closer to their community members, rather than creating a divided "us vs. them" mentality, which is far too often the case when it comes to law enforcement agencies and their communities.

They cooperated with the criminal investigation and initiated their own internal investigation into the matter. Through these actions, they proved that the fact that the alleged offender was a fellow police officer had no bearing. If a crime was committed, then they would do what was right, no matter who was responsible.

They showed true leadership. They owned the story and led the management of this crisis with emotional intelligence. They positioned themselves as the leaders that the community needed to heal and move forward, together.

As could be expected, not all replies and comments about the situation and MVPD were positive. Some community members used this opportunity to share their own negative experiences with Mountain View officers. But the Mountain View Police chose to issue-manage in real time by replying to every single negative comment, just as they did the positive ones, asking people to come forth with their grievances so they could work together to rectify them.

They sustained and strengthened their reputation and the relationships they shared with their community. MVPD and its community grew closer, not apart, through the management of this crisis, which considering the predicament was an extremely honorable feat.

The right mindset, combined with deep-rooted trust, can change everything. It will help you build crisis-resiliency, preventing crises before they can occur, just as it will help you make the right decisions when managing the unpreventable crises that do occur.

You can have the best crisis plan document in the world, but without the right mindset it won't work. People will see right through you. And a big part of this mindset—as well as your crisis ready program—is to find ways to take proactive initiatives to make deposits into your own bank of stakeholder trust every day.

So, before we close this chapter and move on to the next step in your crisis preparedness, I want you to think of three ways your organization—in any, or better yet each, of your departments—can take small actions or find small opportunities in their day-to-day to strengthen the trust between your brand and its stakeholders. These actions should be something different from the initiatives you're already taking. Take a moment to brainstorm three ideas now and jot them down. Writing them here makes you more accountable for their implementation.

Go ahead, I'll wait.

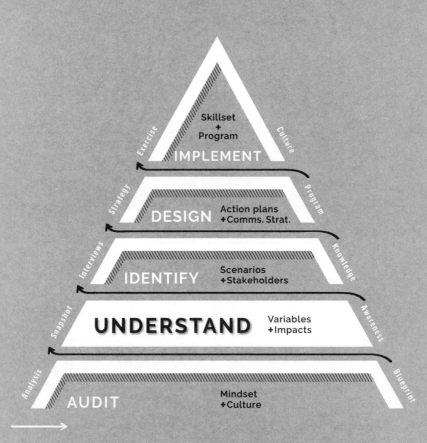

02

LIVING IN THE REAL WORLD

In the summer of 2014, the staff at Emory University Hospital faced a major challenge. But it was a challenge they were ready for.

They had trained with the Centers for Disease Control and Prevention (CDC). Their entire staff knew the protocol. They even had a specialized isolated unit specifically prepared. They were ready to fight Ebola. And they were proud when they learned that they would be the first

American hospital to have the opportunity to do so when two American missionary doctors, who had been stationed in West Africa and unfortunately contracted the disease, were flown to their hospital for care.

Emory has a pronounced presence within their community and is active and engaged on social media. Therefore, after learning the news, they took the natural next step: they leveraged their channels to communicate this important announcement to their community. Except they never expected what was to come next.

Within mere minutes, social media was lighting up with comments—but not the types of comments Emory had anticipated. People were posting messages that said things like, "You're bringing the plague into America!" and, "Shame, shame, shame on you!"

Meanwhile, their inbox was being flooded with what felt like hundreds of emails by the minute, and there were prominent leaders and celebrities taking to Twitter to voice their discontent—tweets that were garnering thousands upon thousands of retweets. All the while, the media was helping the story go viral in a way that magnified the fear and disdain the country seemed to be feeling and openly expressing against Emory.

The staff at Emory University Hospital was blindsided. Here they were, excited to share an announcement for which they were proud and honored, and instead of their community *sharing* in that pride, what felt like the entire country was coming down on them, flooding their channels, and taking what was meant to be a positive story and turning it negatively viral. Emory was cast in a poor light in both traditional and social media. This was not just an annoyance; it was detracting from Emory's ability to get their important message out, and risked impacting the hospital's credibility and reputation within their community and beyond.

What would you do if you were in this type of escalating situation? Do you feel confident that your team would know exactly what to do to communicate through the noise and reclaim the narrative of the situation? Or would it be more of an *ad hoc* effort, reactive but not enough to regain control? If your answer leans more towards the latter, you are certainly not alone.

REALITY CHECK

The internet is a miraculous thing. It gives us the capacity to transcend borders within milliseconds. We're able to follow debates in the Indian Parliament in real time and make a single click or swipe to produce a live feed, with to-the-second social media commentary, of the latest experimental SpaceX launch. The information power we have at our fingertips today is immense and evolutionary.

The digital landscape presents organizations with countless marketing, PR, and stakeholder engagement opportunities. Unfortunately, there is another side to these wonderful opportunities. These same advantages also present organizations with greater risk and increased challenges when it comes to crisis management, such as managing the noise that makes it increasingly difficult to get ahead of the headlines and discussions and drive the narrative of your own story. That's just the tip of the iceberg.

Whether we like it or not, these risks and challenges touch every single organization, no matter its industry, type, or size. They also unavoidably affect every crisis, no matter its origin (which is partly why I get so annoyed with the term "social media crisis," but more on that a little later).

We need to be ready and willing to tackle these real-time challenges head-on, right from the onset of a crisis. This needs to happen simultaneously, while our team works behind the scenes to manage the actual incident that prompted the crisis in the first place. It's only by being able to adequately manage both ends of the crisis—the behind-the-scenes incident and the outward facing demands of your stakeholders—that you will be in a position to successfully manage a crisis in this hyper-connected, fast-paced world.

Unfortunately, considering the demands stakeholders have of organizations these days, competing priorities can be difficult, though not impossible, to juggle. Thankfully, these challenges can be transformed into crisis management opportunities the likes of which organizations never had access to before. That's a strong and exciting statement, don't you think? I'm talking about taking the challenges, many of which can be overwhelming and intimidating, and leveraging them to your *advantage* in times of crisis!

How do you do this? One of the first steps is to truly understand what these challenges are and, most importantly, the reasons behind them. While most professionals are aware of the existence of many of these challenges and obstacles, in my experience not many truly seek to understand the *why* behind them; yet understanding the *why* is where the power lies. It's where you'll find the hidden advantages and opportunities. So, let's do that, shall we? Let's understand both the *what* and the *why* of the crisis management challenges that inevitably lurk before you.

BE ONE STEP AHEAD

One of my clients, an organization with many different facilities around the world, recently experienced an issue in a very remote area of North America that no one ever really hears about. The issue, which was a minor incident that left a disturbingly foul—yet harmless—smell lingering in the air late one evening, caused upset in this very quaint and remote community. While the community members and local journalists took to the internet to post, report, complain, and discuss the issue with one another, my client's savvy communications team was very quick to draft a statement. This statement transparently addressed the situation and calmed concerns...that is, it *would have* calmed concerns had they released the statement themselves, rather than taking the dated approach of waiting for the local radio station to communicate this brilliant message to the community for them...over twelve hours later.

Gone are the days when you could wait to issue your statement to the press by five o'clock to ensure that your company's response would be included in the day's six o'clock news coverage. Nobody waits for the six o'clock news anymore—not even the news media themselves.

With this age of 24/7 news cycles comes a race for the clock. Journalists, reporters, bloggers, and even citizen journalists are all racing against each other to be the first to publish their story—your story—which often results in a lack of the thorough fact-checking and due diligence that used to be fundamentals of reporting. Not to mention that part of the media's job is to sensationalize stories in a way that gains readership and shares. They do this with their chosen headlines and things like clickbait strategies. These sensationalized stories, and their sometimes-unverified facts and misinformation, can easily give rise to rumors and speculation. The more time you allow for rumors and speculation to circulate, the more you risk losing control of the narrative, and the more damage control you'll be forced to undertake in the future.

Part of your objective in a crisis is to always be one step ahead. Sometimes this means your ideal response timeframe is fifteen minutes, while other times you might have a little more leeway. Both timelines are possible to achieve with the right preparedness (ahem, reading this book!), and it's by doing this effectively that you will begin to establish your organization as trustworthy and credible when it matters most. It also enables you to feed the media the story to run with, with the advantage that your organization's key message points will provide consistency and accuracy.

But when time and the rest of the world is racing against you, how can you do this without getting overwhelmed by the need for immediacy? How do you avoid publishing unverified facts yourself while in a scramble to get ahead? There's a fine balance between crisis communication timeliness and accuracy today, and your crisis preparedness needs to enable you to successfully meet that balance.

CRISIS READY RULE

You can't outrun the Internet. You have to outsmart it.

IT DOESN'T HAVE TO BE TRUE

Perception is reality, and fake news is a rising trend. Sometimes it results in irritating issues that can quickly be put to bed with the right timely response (remember the Photoshopped image of the Fisher Price "Happy Hour Playset" that quickly garnered attention?). Other times, fake news can play on people's emotions to the point of potentially helping to sway election votes.

Depending on the situation, fake news, rumors, and speculation can present an issue or a potential crisis. What's important is to be aware that just because something is not true, doesn't mean people won't believe it. This means you should be aware of the impact perception risks having on your brand in different situations so that detection and an appropriate response from your organization can happen swiftly.

THERE'S NO SUCH THING AS A REGIONAL CRISIS

As I mentioned earlier, due to social media and search engines, news today has the capacity to cross oceans in milliseconds. Because of this, there is categorically no longer such thing as a "regional crisis."

Sure, there are crises that affect particular communities and little else. But the reality today is that while these crises will be unavoidably written about in local media, the stories will be published online because every media outlet has an online presence. The second something is published online, its reach becomes instantaneously global. While a regional crisis may be of little to no interest to people outside of the impacted region, the fact is that once something is published online it goes down in search engine history, ready to be retrieved or rediscovered globally at any point now or in the future. This means that future prospective investors, customers, reporters, or anyone else with an interest in your organization can easily find details about the crisis and your response to it.

As a result, there is no way to keep a regional crisis completely within its regional borders. All crises have instantaneous global reach that threatens to affect your organization—for better or worse—at any time.

THERE WILL BE NOISE

Even if you're quick to issue your statement, you still need to find a way to get it heard through the noise. When crisis or controversy strikes, there will be discussions, comments, and questions on social media. Sensationalized headlines may be published and then shared and discussed. Stakeholders will inundate you with calls and emails. The noise that you need to be prepared to rise above can be both overwhelming and unrelenting; yet you have no choice but to ensure that you're heard through it all—that is, if you want your communication efforts to be effective.

To give you some perspective of the possible depth of this noise I'm referring to, let's look at the tragic events that took place on April 15th, 2013, when two terrorist brothers detonated two bombs close to the finish line of the Boston Marathon. Within just the first three hours from the time the bombs went off, there were more than 500,000 tweets with the hashtag #bostonmarathon being published to Twitter. That's half a million tweets with this one hashtag. This doesn't account for tweets with different hashtags, the tweets that didn't include hashtags, the Facebook posts, the YouTube videos, the news articles, the blog posts, the Instagram pictures, and everything else that was being published and shared across the web in real time during this devastating terrorist attack. That's a significant amount of noise that the authorities had to rise above in order for their important updates, directives, and calls to actions to be heard.

This challenging, yet critical, task was instantaneous, and yet the repercussions of *not* communicating in a capacity that would be heard and helpful to the public could mean the difference between life and death in this particular crisis scenario. Thankfully, the Boston Police Department was prepared and had the instincts to activate their social media channels within five minutes from the time the bombs went off. Within the first five minutes of this devastating crisis taking place, Superintendent-in-Chief Daniel Linskey gave his team the following order:

> I need somebody up there to get on social media and let people know what we're doing here, that we're sweeping the streets to make sure it's safe first, and then we'll get them out of the bars, once we get it swept."[5]

Because of Linskey's instinct and direct orders, Boston PD didn't simply position the organization as a source of news and updates throughout the management of this crisis; they were able to position themselves as *the* credible source of news and information regarding and throughout the management of this crisis. No one—not even the media—published information or updates throughout the management of this terrorist attack without first verifying them on Boston PD's channels.

We live in a society where people seem to have this insatiable urge to share everything they experience, as they experience it, online. As a result, today's crises involve a lot of real-time noise, some of which you can expect to be aimed directly at your organization (people will have questions, comments, and points of views that they feel inclined to share), while some of the noise will simply be *about* your organization and the crisis. As we saw above, some of it will be based on fact and some of it will be pure speculation based on rumors, perception, and emotion. But one thing's for sure: you will be expected to hear all of it, acknowledge it, and respond—not to everything, but to the important things that can directly impact the outcome of the crisis and your organization. And the sooner you do this, the less trust and credibility you risk losing, and the more opportunity you have to be the leader of your own crisis.

If Boston PD can manage to successfully overcome the noise in one of the most devastating and chaotic types of crises, there's no reason why your organization can't be in a position to achieve the same.

YOUR RESPONSIBILITY IS TO THEM AND NOT TO YOU

Another reality and challenge these days is that the baseline of expectations that your stakeholders have of your organization, both in and out of a crisis, begins much higher than it ever did before.

It started in 2009 with *United Breaks Guitars* and the infamous Domino's Pizza fiasco. With the impact that consumers had on these brands during these two events, people began to realize the powerful force that their individual and collective voices could have on organizations. It meant that stakeholders no longer needed to tolerate unacceptable behavior, or the once-typical "no comment" response from organizations. Social media and technology have given every person a platform to voice his or her grievances, upset, and discontent in a powerful way. As a result, today's stakeholders expect more of your organization in a crisis, right from the start.

In fact, while we used to be able to refer to these expectations as "expectations", over the last few years, I've watched as they have evolved into *demands*. Demands that, when unmet, can result in an irreparable loss of brand equity, trust, and reputation.

At the bare minimum in a crisis, your stakeholders demand that you listen; they demand to be heard and acknowledged, and for their emotions to be validated; and they demand a compassionate, transparent, and credible response from your organization in an acceptable timeframe. This is a lot to demand, with a lot at stake, but if you want to successfully manage the next crisis that strikes your organization, you need to be prepared to adequately meet these demands.

United Breaks Guitars *is a series of three music videos that were published to YouTube. In these videos, singer song-writer Dave Carroll tells the story of how United Airlines broke his Taylor guitar and didn't care. When Carroll published this video series in 2009, the videos garnered so much attention and outrage, and United's response was so poor, that it dropped the organization's market capitalization by 10%—equal to a CRP of $180 million in value—for a period of time in 2009.*[6]

The infamous Domino's Pizza fiasco occurred when two Domino's Pizza employees published a video to YouTube of them doing disgusting things to some orders before they went out for delivery. The outrage at these videos was so intense, and the impact of the lost trust in the Conover, NC, restaurant where the videos were recorded, was so strong that the restaurant closed its doors for good a few months later. Additionally, the YouTube videos cost Domino's Pizza an estimated one to two percent in sales, nationwide.[7]

WHAT THEY FEEL BEATS WHAT THEY THINK

Emotions run high in times of crisis, both internally and externally. Internally, the team is dealing with the stress of managing the crisis and the fear of the repercussions the crisis threatens to have on the organization. Externally, people are upset, whether directly against your organization or with the circumstances of the situation at large. In either and both cases, emotion makes things messy. Before you know it, people can be tossing around water coolers and writing entire treatises on Twitter!

In fact, one of the biggest fears I see organizations express is, "what if something goes negatively viral against us?" This fear is often one of the biggest reasons why organizations place extremely tight reins on their team's use of social media in general, never mind in a crisis. Of course, having something go negatively viral against your organization is indeed a scary thought. Just ask United Airlines about the time the video of Dr. Dao, a paying customer, being physically abused and literally dragged off the plane by security so that United staff members could take his seat, went viral.

The video of this incident went viral on a global scale in April of 2017, drawing outrage and trending around the world, including in China, Vietnam, and North America. As a result, the incident garnered the attention of Congress, which led to twenty-one Democratic U.S. Senators individually writing to United's CEO, Oscar Munoz, expressing their "deep concern" about the situation. At the time of this writing, some U.S. senators were in the process of working to change legislation and draft acts with the goal of no longer permitting airlines to involuntarily bump paying passengers from overbooked flights.[8]

Additionally, as a direct result of the incident, it was reported that Munoz's employment agreement had been amended to reflect that he would no longer become chairman of the airline, as had previously been the intent.

So yes, negative virality can be a very scary thought. But while we can never guarantee that something will go viral, we *can* identify the risk of something that is *likely* to go viral in a negative way, simply by understanding the effect of emotion.

For example, there's no acceptable reason why United Airlines didn't anticipate that this video of Dr. Dao would go viral and that, when it did, people would be outraged. Had the airline been crisis ready, they would have identified the video as a major risk and would have been prepared to respond *much* better than they did. Instead, it took the airline two days to issue an appropriate statement of apology and commitment to do and be better—and this was after a couple previous inadequate statements had been published both publicly and internally.

With the attention the video garnered, combined with the airline's inadequate first responses, by Tuesday, April 11[9], 2017, two days after the incident occurred and the viral video was published online, United's market capitalization fell by $1.4 billion[9] in pre-market trading.

> If we look at this through the filter of the airline's Crisis Response Penalty, the CRP was $1.4 billion divided by 2 days, making it about $700 million per day. That's an expensive mistake—and that's not even factoring the above mentioned impacts in addition to this!

What would have happened if United had been smart enough to anticipate the impact of the video, and adequately respond in a more acceptable timeframe? People would have still been upset at the situation, and the story would have still gone viral, but United could have been in a better position to mitigate many of the dire consequences they experienced. (Though let's be real here, had United *really* been crisis ready, this incident would never have happened in the first place.)

The truth is that the risk or fear is misplaced when it's directed at virality. The real risks lie in underestimating the impact of emotion and

**CRISIS
READY RULE**

Always assume
there's video.

attempting to trump emotion with logic. Doing either of these things will be a big part of your crisis management downfall—not the fact that something went negatively viral against your brand.

UNDERSTANDING EMOTION

In order to be able to identify the potential of something going viral against your organization, you need to understand, first, that virality is relative to your organization's "normal." For example, virality doesn't have to mean 500,000 tweets in a day. It can mean 50 or 500 shares and mentions in a day, or over the span of a couple of days. The measure of virality depends on the benchmarks of your organization's normal online activity and the potential impact the situation risks having on your brand.

The second thing to understand is what makes something go viral in the first place. What is it that prompts someone to click "like," "share," or "RT" to a piece of content? After all, the term "viral" is defined as "an image, video, piece of information, etc., that is circulated rapidly and widely from one Internet user to another."[10] So, the question is what makes something worthy of being "circulated rapidly and widely?"

There are three components that are consistently found in each piece of viral content. These three components are:

1. An emotionally compelling story;

2. Relatability; and

3. Shareable format.

When you're identifying and assessing a risk, you want your team to instinctively look for a combination of these three components. None of these things on their own will prompt something to go viral, but combine them together and you'll get a story, article, video, or picture that people will be inclined to share. And the more it gets shared, the more it has the potential to go viral. Let's make this real with an example.

Boko Haram, an Islamic extremist group based in Nigeria, has been tormenting and murdering innocent men, women, and children for years. In January 2015, the terrorist group brutally slaughtered two-thousand innocent Nigerians in what was called their "deadliest massacre."[11] Even though some of the biggest media outlets reported on the incident and shared devastating photos of the attack, the event only garnered a small amount of attention from the western world with little conversation about it on social media before the media was onto their next story and people continued with their daily lives.

A few days later, on January 7th, 2015, two brothers barged into the headquarters of the French satirical newspaper, *Charlie Hebdo*, in Paris, and shot and killed twelve people while wounding eleven others. But unlike the Boko Haram massacre, this attack went viral in a way that united the world. The hashtag #JeSuisCharlie (#IamCharlie) quickly became one of the most used news hashtags in Twitter's history at the time,[12] and four days after the attack two million people, including over forty world leaders, stood arm in arm to rally together in Paris, while millions of others joined in the movement throughout major cities around the world.[13]

What was it that made the impact and the viral nature of these two devastating events so different? Both were heinous acts. One resulted in two-thousand innocent people being slaughtered, while the other resulted in the murder of twelve innocent people. So then why did the Charlie Hebdo attack go viral while the Boko Haram slaughter went nearly unnoticed?

One could argue that both attacks happened near the same time, so one took the spotlight more than the other; or that more media outlets reported on the attack in Paris, versus the slaughter in Nigeria. But Boko Haram has been

CRISIS READY RULE

Emotion always overpowers reason.

brutally murdering and terrorizing Nigerians for years and there are many credible news sources that report on these devastating incidents when they happen. And yet, the news of these terrible events has never garnered nearly the same amount of attention or reaction from the western world as the Charlie Hebdo attack did. So, if it has nothing to do with the timing of the events or the amount of media outlets that report on them, let's compare both events against our three components of viral content:

1. An emotionally compelling story

Both events are emotionally compelling. Murder, slaughter, and terrorist attacks are always emotionally compelling stories. When you compare the photography of these two events, one might even be more inclined to say that the images of dozens and hundreds of bodies lying in the dirt are more emotionally compelling than the pictures that surfaced from the Charlie Hebdo attack. So, while both events have this attribute of virality, let's look at how they differ in their other two attributes.

2. Relatability

This is where the attacks begin to differ. While the Boko Haram slaughter is a devastating story, the reality is that the western world has a hard time relating to it. We have difficulty seeing ourselves in this story further than in our most horrifying nightmares, and fortunately, these are nightmares that we're blessed to be able to wake up from. This story isn't our reality. It is therefore difficult to relate to a country and to people who live this horror day in and day out.

On the other hand, the attack on Charlie Hebdo happened in our backyard. It happened to our neighbors. We can easily relate to this event and it scares the crap out of us. We can put ourselves in the victims' shoes and imagine someone barging into our place of work and threatening our safety. And worse yet, this attack touched us on an even deeper level because it attempted to threaten our freedom of press and our freedom of expression—one of the core values of western civilization. However, as a global community, we refused to be silenced. This was an aspect of this incident that united us on an extremely emotional and relatable level.

3. Shareable format

Less than an hour after the shooting, an image of the words "Je Suis Charlie" (I am Charlie) was shared to Twitter by Joachim Roncin, the artistic director of Stylist Magazine. These three short words, which were quickly transformed into a hashtag, amplified the emotional relatability of this event by bringing us all, individually, into the story. Roncin told Huffington Post,[14] "I wanted to communicate that this affected me. I feel personally targeted. It kills me, you know." And he certainly wasn't alone in feeling this way.

This short and catchy phrase put into words the emotions that millions of people around the world were feeling at that very moment. It wasn't "you are Charlie," nor was it "they are Charlie." It was "*I* am Charlie." It brought each and every one of us, individually and collectively, into the horror that we could already relate to on a profoundly emotional level. In fact, this phrase was so catchy and relatable that, within several hours, the hashtag #JeSuisCharlie had been tweeted more than 600,000 times,[14] and over the course of the next few days it was used in print media, in cartoons including *The Simpsons* and *Charlie Brown*, and was incorporated into music. A town square in France was even renamed "Je Suis Charlie."

An emotionally compelling story, dowsed in relatability and enveloped in a shareable format, is an extremely powerful combination (in the case of *Je Suis Charlie*, the sharable format was three words that became a hashtag).

When used against your organization, you're facing a high potential for a very quick escalation of an issue or a crisis. The digital landscape has amplified this impactful risk in crisis management. Every member of your team should be aware of this reality, as detection can come from anywhere within your organization.

You can never know for certain where an issue or crisis is going to originate and who will be the first person to detect it. Part of implementing a crisis ready culture means that no matter where a crisis originates, or who detects it, your team is trained and empowered to first identify it as a risk, and then to quickly assess its immediate potential impact, initiating its escalation as required. Part of doing this means being able to determine whether the situation has, or risks having, an emotionally relatable attribute that may help it quickly escalate.

One tip I provide clients when helping them train their teams to be versed in the detection of a given situation's emotional impact, is to create a series of questions that the person or people who first detect the threat will use to help them determine whether the incident needs to be escalated internally.

Following is an example of what these questions might look like. Feel free to take them and adapt them to better suit your organization.

Evaluate the emotional relatability of a negative situation

☐ Is this story / image / video emotionally compelling? i.e., does it evoke a strong human emotion?

☐ Is this story / image / video highly relatable on an emotional level? i.e., can you easily relate to this story, or are others likely to relate to this story?

☐ If people were inclined to share this story / image / video with their friends, family or network, does it have a high likelihood to provoke a negative reaction or sentiment towards the organization, or one of its key representatives?

If you answer "yes" to each of the following questions, immediately report the incident to your manager, in order for them to evaluate the potential impact of the situation and decide on an appropriate response.

Had the United Airlines team been versed in this type of understanding of emotional relatability, and had the organization had a protocol of this sort, do you think the airline would have waited hours before responding (horribly) to the video of Dr. Dao's abuse? Or do you think they would have been able to quickly detect the evident risk of this situation, enabling them to react and respond far better than they did?

The key to understanding viral content is to understand the human nature behind what makes something go viral. Use this information to teach your teams to quickly identify these sorts of risks before they escalate beyond a point of control.

EVERYBODY IS AT RISK OF A CRISIS

Technology has leveled the playing field. We've seen large global organizations, just as we've seen small local shops and personal brands, get destroyed by the crisis management challenges that have become our reality. This means that, no matter the size of your organization, everything we've discussed throughout this chapter—and everything we have yet to discuss throughout this book—directly applies to you, your team and your business.

Don't believe me? Just ask Justine Sacco or Union Street Guest House. In December of 2013, Sacco, who was the senior director of corporate communications at IAC at the time, tweeted the following tweet to her 170 followers a short while before boarding her eleven-hour flight to Cape Town, South Africa:

 Going to Africa. Hope I don't get AIDS. Just kidding. I'm white!"

It's important to mention that Sacco didn't mean this as a racially profane or ignorant comment. In fact, she later explained to a reporter of the *New York Times*[15] that

Only an insane person would think that white people don't get AIDS."
She continued to explain, saying "to me it was so insane of a comment
for anyone to make. I thought there was no way that anyone could
possibly think it was literal."

But none of that mattered. For two big reasons.

1. Sacco was not there to take control of the narrative, explain her
   intent or apologize in real-time, as she was isolated to her eleven-
   hour flight; and

2. Truth be told, this type of comment is not redeemable, no matter
   what the context or intention may be—especially confined to 140
   characters, or after eleven hours!

By the time Sacco's flight landed in Cape Town and she turned her phone
back on, her tweet had gone wildly viral with tens of thousands of angry
responses tweeted back to her. She also quickly learned that her handle,
@Justine-Sacco, was the number one worldwide trend on Twitter. Not to
mention that the hashtag #HasJustineLandedYet had garnered so much global
attention that someone in Cape Town actually went to the airport just to snap
a picture of her and tweeted "Yup @JustineSacco HAS in fact landed at Cape
Town International. She's decided to wear sunnies as a disguise." Furthermore,
this tweet and its escalation lost Sacco her job.

One tweet, posted with poor judgement and an inability to respond for
eleven hours, resulted in a full-blown crisis for this otherwise accomplished
professional. A crisis that lasted for several months (if not years) and
impacted her reputation, both professionally and personally, her career,
and her livelihood.

> I don't know what Sacco's salary was, but if we filter this crisis through the CRP lens, the eleven hours that Sacco was unable to respond to the incident resulted in a major hourly CRP! *(CRP = Sacco's annual salary divided by eleven hours)*

What about Union Street Guest House, you ask? Union Street Guest House, once a boutique hotel located in Hudson, New York, faced outrage in 2014 when *Page Six*[16] of *The New York Post* reported that this quaint inn had a policy on their website that declared they would charge guests a $500 fine for every bad review published online about the inn. To be exact, their website policy read:

> " If you have booked the Inn for a wedding or other type of event anywhere in the region and given us a deposit of any kind for guests to stay at USGH there will be a $500 fine that will be deducted from your deposit for every negative review of USGH placed on any internet site by anyone in your party and / or attending your wedding or event. If you stay here to attend a wedding anywhere in the area and leave us a negative review on any internet site you agree to a $500 fine for each negative review."

If you've ever read *Hug Your Haters*, by Jay Baer (and if you haven't, you should), then you'll know that research and real life dictates that this is the exact opposite approach to take with negative reviews against your business! Can you guess what happened next to this otherwise reputable inn? The day after the article, the inn's Facebook page and Yelp were inundated with over 3,000 negative reviews.

Chris Wagoner, the owner of the inn, quickly addressed the issue with an explanation and an apology, and promptly removed the policy from their website. Unfortunately, the damage had already been done. These long-lasting negative online reviews permanently affected the brand's once solid and respectable reputation.

At the time of this writing, three years after the *Page Six* article, a quick search on Google for "Union Street Guest House" showed me a full page of results discussing nothing about this inn, other than the fact that they tried to fine customers $500 for negative online reviews. Furthermore, the very first result on Google was a Yelp result, with the title, "Union Street Guest House - CLOSED - 14 Photos & 98 Reviews ... - Yelp."

Negative reviews in overwhelming numbers tarnished this hotel's reputation so profoundly that it is no longer in business. This tongue and cheek "joke" policy, as Wagoner described it at the time, was a sorry mistake that lead to irreparable consequences.

> **The soft CRP, i.e., the long-lasting reputational impact, in this case was detrimental.**

No matter your organization's size, type, or industry, these real-world crisis management realities apply to you. However, there is a positive twist!

The positive twist is that all these real-time risks and challenges also present you with unprecedented opportunities for crisis and issue management. Opportunities that also apply to all organizations. The big, the small, the private, the public, the for-profit, the not-for-profit, and everything in between.

For example, on one hand, the news cycle may be a challenging 24/7 phenomenon, but on the other hand your organization—no matter its size or type—now possesses the ability to be its own real-time media. Leverage this well and you are no longer dependent on the media or their narrative. Instead, you can position your organization as the credible source of information and updates throughout the management of your own crisis. And while it may be difficult to filter through and rise above the noise, mobile technology gives you the opportunity to streamline your communications, bypassing the noise and reaching your target audience directly in their pockets.

The digital landscape can present many scary new challenges when it comes to crisis management, but it also presents unprecedented opportunities for that very same crisis management. And the best part is that everyone has access to these same tools, technologies, and opportunities. In fact, for the most part they are free! It's just a matter of knowing how to use them to your advantage.

LEADERSHIP'S ROLE

In order to implement a crisis ready culture, let's face it, the organization needs full buy-in from, and support of, leadership. Not only is culture implemented from the top down, but without this buy-in and support, resistance is bound to get in the way, which won't help in mitigating (never mind managing) a crisis. So, before we close out this chapter, let's discuss some of the biggest, most common internal obstacles that organizations face when seeking that buy-in, along with some strategic steps you can take to overcome them. Whether you're a member of the leadership team, or a manager or director seeking to gain full buy-in from leadership, the following will serve and support this effort.

There are several common reasons behind the resistance that many professionals experience, when trying to sell the need to be crisis ready. Depending on your organization and its culture, this resistance can stem from things like:

• Management wrongfully believes that the old ways of managing crises still apply and will continue to work for the organization.

• The organization feels immune to crises.

- Certain departments (e.g., legal) or executives have a hard time releasing the reins and being open to the need to be proactive and communicate in a timely fashion in times of crisis.

- The organization lacks the necessary resources to dedicate to this type of initiative.

Do any of these sound familiar?

These internal blocks can be frustrating for team members who understand that the organization is vulnerable and insufficiently prepared to successfully manage crises. I've seen just how frustrating this can be for forward-thinking professionals. There are three ways to approach overcoming this internal obstacle and gaining the required buy-in. One or a combination of the following three approaches may work for you and your objectives, depending on the people you're trying to sway.

APPROACH #1: ASK TWO IMPORTANT QUESTIONS

In chapter four we'll discuss your organization's high-risk scenarios, but before we get there, following is an exercise to consider undertaking with different members of your leadership team. This exercise will help you spark discussions and gain necessary awareness. The exercise is as follows:

Ask each member of management what type of risk or crisis scenario keeps them up at night. Then, using some of the crisis management challenges we've discussed in this chapter, present them with the obstacles the organization would be faced with in the event of these scenarios. Ask them if they think the organization would be able to successfully overcome these challenges.

Each member of management will have a different crisis scenario in mind, depending on what his or her position and responsibilities are within the organization. For example, your head of HR may be worried about workplace violence or employee misconduct, while your Chief Information Officer will be thinking more about cybersecurity threats. For this reason, and to achieve the best results, I recommend conducting this exercise in a group setting, where it will be collaborative. Each person who raises their concerns will add to the last concern expressed, helping management realize that there are multiple risks and challenges that the organization may not necessarily be ready for.

APPROACH #2: EDUCATE (AND SCARE A LITTLE!)

As a crisis management strategist and keynote speaker, I've learned that there's a beneficial way to use both of my skill sets to help educate management teams regarding today's crisis management realities. Look at this as an internal keynote presentation for your management team, where the objective is to educate, provoke thought, and inspire action, ultimately getting you that buy-in.

This should be an interactive presentation (an hour or two long) that discusses the realities of today's crisis management. Use real-world examples of organizations that have managed them well, as well as others who have failed. It should also provide the team with some simple steps that they could begin taking to implement a crisis ready culture, helping them realize that this objective is a realistic one to attain, rather than being an overwhelming endeavor that will consume all their time.

Oftentimes, bringing in an outside expert with real-world experience helps to bring a level of credibility that offers additional weight and support to your objectives. If this is an approach that might work with your team, following are some recommendations to help you hire the right professional.

- The person you hire should be a talented speaker with real-world crisis management and preparedness experience. The talented speaker aspect will make it an entertaining and engaging experience, while the real-world experience will bring the required credibility you'll need to really make an impact.

- Make sure it's not a sales pitch. Too often, I hear from clients that the consultants and / or speakers they hired before me used these opportunities to pitch and sell further services. Make sure this doesn't happen to you. (If you happen to be a consultant reading this book, don't do this!) It will only detract from the important message and impact you're aiming to achieve. Instead, this should be viewed as a worthy project or deliverable in and of itself. Not a way to get more business! The professional you choose should be passionate about delivering this message. If they do it well, maybe you'll choose to hire them for more work and maybe you won't. Their goal with this presentation should be to help you achieve your internal objectives, nothing more.

APPROACH #3: TEST THE TEAM

If management feels they're ready to handle a crisis, then why not put them—and your current crisis plan—to the test? While crisis simulations make great training exercises once an organization has developed their crisis ready program, they can also be a stimulating way to help you gain that buy-in. (Spoiler alert! We will discuss crisis simulations in detail in chapter nine, where I will help you develop a realistic scenario and successfully conduct this wonderful exercise.)

A crisis simulation is an exercise that feels as though a real crisis is unfolding, even though it takes place in a controlled and safe environment. During this exercise, the crisis management team is given a few hours to successfully (or unsuccessfully) manage the unfolding crisis. This type of exercise offers more than a traditional tabletop. Unlike a traditional tabletop where a scenario is presented and then discussed, a simulation is an interactive exercise where the team encounters the real-world challenges we've highlighted throughout this chapter, and must get up and take the right actions to manage the unfolding, simulated crisis.

This type of exercise can be one of the most effective ways to gain buy-in, due to its level of realism. The scenario and its challenges are realistic, and the results and impact are immediately felt. In my experience, it's always been a highly effective exercise that helps to educate, create awareness, and motivate next steps!

How did Emory fare in managing their viral situation?

Even though the staff at Emory University Hospital may have been blindsided by the fallout of their Ebola announcement, they are so crisis ready that they instinctively knew how to handle this viral situation. So, what did they do?

First, they quickly assessed the situation and sought to understand the reason behind what was happening. Why were people reacting and responding in such an intensely negative way? Through reading and truly *listening* to what people were expressing, the staff at Emory quickly realized that this reaction was a result of two things:

1. People didn't understand how Ebola is spread; and

2. Their community didn't know just how prepared Emory truly was to care for Ebola patients.

You see, there is a potential crisis within the crisis of Ebola, and it's called FEAR-BOLA. Fear-bola is a very real phenomenon, and it's what we were beginning to see following Emory's announcement. Fear-bola is the irrational fear of Ebola. As we saw in our discussion about emotion, Fear-bola is based purely in emotion. Logic has nothing to do with it. And this emotion is extremely powerful.

Think of it. Emory was receiving messages saying they were bringing the plague into the country. That's an incredibly strong statement. What Americans knew of Ebola was that it was uncontrollably spreading and killing more and more people in West Africa. Even the doctors who went to help clearly couldn't protect themselves. And now Emory was *willingly* bringing this plague-like disease to America? Are they crazy? What could they possibly be thinking?

Combine this irrational fear with the fact that people didn't realize just how prepared Emory was to care for Ebola-stricken patients. They had trained with the CDC for months. Their entire staff knew the protocol, and they had a special containment unit ready and dedicated to caring for Ebola patients.

So, armed with an understanding of the *why*, Emory knew the answer to this viral issue was that people needed to be properly informed about the disease and Emory's level of preparedness. But they also knew that the strong emotion the nation was feeling could not simply be trumped by logical explanations. So, they sought to communicate in a way that was emotionally relatable.

Over the course of the next few days, Emory published videos[17] of qualified staff members, dressed in lab coats, addressing and answering the key concerns that people were expressing. These qualified staff members didn't just speak in medical jargon, they communicated their important messages and information in a very human, relatable, and visual way that all viewers would trust and understand.

Emory also continuously published informative FAQs[18] and other content[19] that focused on educating the public about Ebola, how it spreads, and why Emory was so confident in their ability to successfully care for these Ebola patients. Additionally, the head nurse at Emory published an article titled, "I'm the head nurse at Emory. This is why we wanted to bring the Ebola patients to the U.S." to the *Washington Post*,[20] in a successful attempt to be personable and extend the reach of Emory's message on a trusted third party platform.

And it all worked. By understanding the why behind what was happening, the expectations of their stakeholders, and understanding the emotional impact of the situation, and by choosing to use all this information to release a series of timely and adequate responses, Emory quickly regained control of the narrative of the story, and positioned itself as the credible leader of the situation. Almost immediately, the messages that Emory was receiving turned from negative to positive. People were now thanking Emory for their leadership and compassion, saying things like "Emory is the best!" and "Thank you so much for taking care of those two folks who have sacrificed so much..."

Emory was clearly ready for the real-time challenges that this situation presented, and even though they were blindsided by the way the situation escalated, they had the right instincts and training to quickly assess and manage this viral issue. They were crisis ready.

Because of Emory's swift and adequate response, the organization suffered zero CRP.

Would your team have been able to know instinctively how to respond in the same capacity that Emory did? If not, then gain that buy-in, educate your team on the realities and challenges that await your organization in times of crisis, and continue reading!

Don't worry. You'll get there. We're going to make sure of it!

03

PEOPLE
FIRST

On Thursday, October 15th, 2015, the CEO of United Airlines, Oscar Munoz, suffered a heart attack and was rushed to the hospital. As a result, United postponed a labor summit with union leaders that had been on the calendar for months. They chose not to disclose the reason for the postponement, citing simply a "personal emergency." The next day, the *Wall Street Journal* was one of the first media outlets to report on the fact that Munoz was in the hospital because of a heart attack.

In the wake of the initial media reports that followed, United's stock price began to drop. By close on Friday, the price had plummeted 3%. The airline finally decided to issue the following statement, released in the early afternoon of Friday, October 16th:

> CHICAGO, Oct. 16, 2015 /PRNewswire/ — We have been informed by Oscar's family that he was admitted to the hospital on Thursday and we will provide further details as appropriate. In the meantime, we are continuing to operate normally.
>
> Our thoughts and prayers are with his family and we are respecting their privacy."

Before continuing further, take a moment to jot down your initial thoughts about this statement. Had you received this statement as a stakeholder of United, what would you have thought? What sentiment would you have felt towards United?

_____

_____

_____

_____

_____

_____

Great! We'll come back to your reflections towards the end of this chapter.

Strong businesses are built on the prioritization of their key relationships. Without these relationships, your organization would cease to exist. Not to mention that you have worked hard to build the relationships you have with your key stakeholders. It has been an ongoing initiative since the beginning of your business, your professional career...whatever the case may be.

As we discussed in chapter one, the right crisis mindset prioritizes people over processes and bottom lines. If your priorities are not in the right place, not only will you be more issue- and crisis-prone, but people will feel that they are not your priority and you will end up losing—losing trust, losing credibility and, ultimately, losing those relationships. And once lost, these things are not easily regained.

Stakeholders expect a lot from today's organizations. Put yourself in their shoes and look at what you expect from the brands you engage with or purchase from. If you communicate with them, whether it be via a tweet, a phone call, an email (especially out of frustration), do you expect a response? How quickly do you expect that response? Within hours? Minutes? *Seconds?* What do you expect of that response? Do you expect to be validated and for your concerns to be heard and addressed? For your questions to be answered? Do you expect the organization to actually *care?* Do you hope that something positive will come out of the engagement? What happens if these expectations are not met? Do you walk away and never look back? I know I sure do! And that's just in the everyday moments. In a crisis, the expectations of stakeholders are amplified. Failing to meet their expectations can result in everything from broken trust, to lost relationships, to the unsuccessful management of the crisis.

In times of crisis, these relationships—and your organization's prioritization of these relationships—will be put to the test. This means that being prepared to meet your stakeholders' expectations in a crisis is mandatory for your organization's crisis management success. However, this is not something you want to just wing and hope to get right; too much is at stake. The demands and

CRISIS READY RULE

When in doubt, focus on (re)building and strengthening relationships.

expectations of your stakeholders in a crisis start at minute zero, and continue to escalate until met. This is one reason why implementing a crisis ready culture is truly the best strategy for success. The goal is to get to a place of crisis preparedness where your team instinctively knows what is expected of them and how to meet those expectations in real time.

To get to this level of organization-wide preparedness, your team will need to arm itself with the following three things:

1. A holistic understanding of who your organization's key stakeholders are;

2. Knowledge of what their demands will be in a crisis; and

3. An ability to meet those expectations in real time.

So, let's aim to give you everything you need to meet—or better yet, exceed—your stakeholders' high demands, even in times when emotions will be running high and time will be of the essence. Meeting the above standards is the foundation of any successful crisis management strategy because when it comes down to it, the relationships you share with your stakeholders are the heart of your business. Nothing can function without its heart.

WHO ARE YOUR MOST IMPORTANT PEOPLE?

Before deciding who your key stakeholders are, let's first define what exactly a stakeholder is. Stakeholders are every person, group of people, or entity that enables your business to operate. Without them, your organization would cease to exist—or at least would cease to *successfully* exist! You have internal stakeholders and external stakeholders, and the first step in meeting their expectations is to identify each category of stakeholder that is pertinent to your business.

This may seem common knowledge, but in my experience, most organizations don't have one centralized, global list of their stakeholder groups. Instead, each department knows whom they have relationships with. In times of crisis, having a centralized list helps ensure that no one important is being overlooked or forgotten in the haste of things.

Take the time now to create this list, and note that there is no room for speculation or guesswork. Making sure you have a solid list of your key stakeholder groups will require conversations with different department, regional, and divisional heads. Additionally, and for best results, while making this list and having these conversations you'll want to understand:

- Which department(s) or function(s) "owns" the relationships with each stakeholder group.

- The means of communication used to communicate with each stakeholder group during day-to-day activities.

- Whether a database currently exists that holds each stakeholder's contact information; who has access to this database; and whether it's backed up in a secondary location in the event of an incident where systems are down, such as a cybersecurity event.

- What each stakeholder group will expect of the organization in times of crisis.

- How prepared the organization currently is at meeting these expectations.

When I start working with a new client, my very first task is to conduct interviews with each "stakeholder owner" to gather this information.

Presumably, you know your business, and probably have an initial understanding of your stakeholder groups, their touch points and expectations. Gathering this information will probably take you less time and effort than it does me when I walk into a new client's office for the first time! However, do not assume you know any of the answers at any time.

To get you started, following are some examples of internal and external stakeholder groups. The ones that apply to your organization depend on the nature of your business.

INTERNAL STAKEHOLDERS

- Board members
- Employees and, by extension, their families
- Trustees
- Volunteers

EXTERNAL STAKEHOLDERS

- Advocates / fans / supporters
- Authorities / government entities
- Candidates
- Contractors
- Counterparties / lenders
- Customers / clients / patients
- General public
- GMOs
- Influencers
- Insurance providers / brokers
- Investors
- Legislators
- Media
- Regulators
- Shareholders
- Union representatives
- Vendors / suppliers

Not every stakeholder within your stakeholder groups will necessarily bear the same weight or importance to the organization; just as some stakeholders are going to have larger expectations, and command a swifter, more personalized response from the organization in times of crisis. For this reason, I recommend dividing your stakeholder groups into two tiers.

For example, if your organization has investors, odds are that some of them are more pertinent to the organization's financial success than others. These investors may *expect* to be notified first in the event of a crisis, and this expectation may be that someone—the person they have a relationship with—will pick up the phone and verbally deliver the news. These are tier one investors. Tier two investors are the remaining investors who, though equally important to communicate with in the event of a crisis, you may not need to call directly. Instead, a well-crafted email may do the trick.

Dividing your stakeholders into tiers helps you better understand their individual expectations of your organization in a crisis, and helps you better manage your team's time and tasks in the initial moments when things are the most hectic.

Earlier, I mentioned the database that houses your stakeholders' contact information. When identifying stakeholders, and having the necessary conversations with those who maintain the organization's relationships with them, you should be thinking about contact information. I often find that some departments have robust systems in place that make life easy when you want to find the contact information for specific individuals, while other departments have contact information in— and only in—their personal mobile devices. I have even spoken with department heads who have told me their key stakeholders' contact information is in their heads—*gasp!* You can imagine how my heart raced thinking of the risk involved with such a storage location!

CRISIS READY RULE

You never know where you will be when crisis strikes. Ensure multiple remotely accessible copies of your program are safely stored.

In the event of a crisis, anybody who may need to communicate with a stakeholder, whether individually or as a collective, needs to be able to. This information should be easily accessible and organized. This will go a long way towards helping you efficiently meet your stakeholders' real-time expectations, and alleviate a lot of stress for your team.

MEETING EXPECTATIONS

Now that you have a clear understanding of who your stakeholders are, your next step is to identify and understand what they will each expect and demand of your organization. The more you understand their expectations, the more you can enable your organization to anticipate and meet them. It is important that you don't guess or assume when undertaking this exercise. Have conversations—with your stakeholders themselves, even—to better understand the actions your teams will need to take.

In my experience, following is a minimum of what you can expect people to expect. While the specific requirements for the following expectations depend on the crisis scenario and the stakeholder group, these eight expectations should be considered a baseline.

1. IN A CRISIS, PEOPLE EXPECT TO BE NOTIFIED

Depending on the type of crisis you are dealing with, notification requirements will vary. Sometimes they will be legally required, as in the case of a cybersecurity event where personally identifiable information (PII) has been stolen. Other times, notification might just constitute a courtesy call or email. Those who matter most to your organization will appreciate the courtesy of hearing the news from you first, rather than from the media, social media, or on the street.

When conducting a deep-dive into your high-risk scenarios, which we will explore in the next chapter, you will want to evaluate each specific scenario, combined with each individual stakeholder group, and determine what the notification requirements and expectations are. This may involve having conversations with each stakeholder owner, your legal department, compliance department, the stakeholders themselves, and any other relevant subject matter experts.

2. IN A CRISIS, PEOPLE EXPECT TRANSPARENCY

If people feel you are hiding or omitting information, they'll turn away from your organization's communications because they won't trust them. This means that any chance of your organization shaping the narrative of its own crisis will be lost, and criticism against your organization will ensue.

However, sometimes it is not easy to be transparent, as there are aspects of a crisis you may not be permitted to share for legal or other reasons. There is also the risk of oversharing. Therefore, while there are different approaches to communicating transparently, depending on the situation, some good rules of thumb are:

- Communicate what you know for sure and are legally allowed to disclose.

- If there are specific details that you have not yet confirmed, or that you are not permitted to disclose, and if you know that people have questions regarding these details or will demand answers, address your restrictions rather than avoiding or omitting them. Be honest with people and let them know what you're doing to gather or verify the information, or that you are not legally or otherwise permitted to share certain information. Confront the situation, rather than avoid it. If you avoid it, you risk facing anything from unnecessary criticism, speculation, and rumors to lost trust and credibility.

CRISIS READY RULE

A mistake can be forgiven. The appearance of a cover-up will not be.

- Whenever you can, take actions that reinforce your transparency. For example, you may consider live-streaming your press conferences or the behind-the-scenes management of the crisis. The more you demonstrate your commitment to transparency, the more you will position your organization as the credible source of information throughout the crisis, and the less stakeholder trust you will lose.

It's not just about the words you communicate, but also the actions you take and are seen taking. A commitment to transparency while managing a crisis is a powerful thing that will not only meet expectations, but help you continue to strengthen the trusting relationships you share with your stakeholders.

3. IN A CRISIS, PEOPLE EXPECT TIMELY, CONSISTENT COMMUNICATION

This is often one of the biggest challenges of crisis management, when crises can be live-streamed and people will expect a response from the organization possibly before you're even aware that a crisis has struck. However, the fact is that the longer you wait to communicate in a crisis, the more risk there is of the crisis spiraling out of control, and the more you risk losing trust and credibility.

The timeline for communication really depends on the scenario. If the crisis is a major one with far reach and impact, then a good rule of thumb is to communicate within fifteen to sixty minutes from the time the crisis develops an online presence. Note that I did *not* say from the time you learn of the situation, which can be an entirely different timeline! The second a crisis develops an online presence, its reach and potential impact significantly increase.

This doesn't give you much time, does it? The good news is that stakeholders will not expect you to have all the answers within the first few minutes of a crisis breaking. What they *will* expect is a response that reassures them that you are aware, that you care, that you're taking the appropriate actions to address the situation, and that you will be committed to timely, consistent, and transparent communications. We call this a "first response statement" and there are things you can do now to make sure you meet the expectation of timeliness. We will discuss these strategies a little later in this book.

On the other hand, sometimes you can put less severe crises and issues to bed quickly with a more thoughtful, complete communication, rather than a first response approach. In these situations, you have a little more time to gather the required information and make one strong, single statement that addresses concerns and closes out the issue. However, even in this context of "more time," I am talking about a few hours, not more. You never want to go for days before issuing a statement, no matter how good the statement is! We will go into more detail regarding these types of situations a little later as well.

4. IN A CRISIS, PEOPLE EXPECT YOU TO LISTEN AND VALIDATE THEIR FEELINGS AND EMOTIONS

Does "validating emotions" sound familiar? As we discussed in chapter two, emotions run high in times of crisis. These emotions, whether you agree with them or not, will be extremely real for the people experiencing them. This means that if you want your message to be heard by emotional people, they need to feel as though you truly care about them, the situation, and its consequences. In order to do this effectively, you need to be ready and willing to listen to, and validate, what they are feeling.

As a result, both your communications and actions need to come from a place of heart and sincerity. You need to show compassion and be ready to sincerely apologize when an apology is merited. This can be difficult for some leaders and their legal departments, but you need to remember that an apology is not an admittance of guilt, and it is an expectation that needs to be met. Let's be real here; when it's the right thing to do, it's the right thing to do!

5. IN A CRISIS, PEOPLE EXPECT TWO-WAY COMMUNICATION

You can thank social media for this one. Gone are the days when you could deliver your statement, turn around, walk away, and go back to managing the incident behind the scenes. Social media has enabled real-time, two-way dialogue, and those of your stakeholders who choose to use these platforms in this capacity will expect you to be there, ready and willing to communicate and respond.

This is another reason for the importance of listening and monitoring, and means that your team needs to know how to triage coverage, concerns, and misinformation. They also need to know when it is appropriate to respond and how to respond in those times, as well as when it is time to sit back and listen, letting the conversation unfold on its own.

In the interest of providing your team with a resource to help them answer these important questions, the following insert is an issue management response flowchart that I have designed. Feel free to download this flowchart for free at http://melissaagnes.com/flowchart and use it as-is, or adapt it to better suit your organization.

6. IN A CRISIS, PEOPLE EXPECT TO BE COMMUNICATED WITH BY HUMAN BEINGS—NOT LAWYERS OR LOGOS

International Paper (IP) is an organization that specializes in manufacturing fiber-based packaging, and pulp and paper. In January of 2017, IP experienced a crisis when their Cantonment, Florida mill suffered an explosion. The explosion released a waste product called black liquor into the environment, affecting communities as far away as ten miles from the site of the explosion. Black liquor covered everything in these communities; the ground, homes, cars, you name it. The day after the explosion, IP finally issued a statement, which read:

MEMPHIS, Tenn., Jan. 23, 2017 /PRNewswire/ — On the evening of Jan. 22, International Paper Company (NYSE: IP) experienced significant structural damage to the largest pulp digester as well as

CRISIS READY™ FLOWCHART

LEGEND
- Sit back and monitor
- Respond accordingly
- Escalate to crisis

NEGA... ISSU... OCCU...

Is it garnering a lot o...

NO

Can we easily c... regain control o...

YES

Does the situation risk escalating further?

NO

YES

Can we easily put the issue to bed with a sincere and honest response?

Does t... negative... reputa... botto... le...

NO

Monitor the situation and let our community come to our defense. Consider responding to individual comments and questions with the aim of strengthening relationships, as required.

NO

YES

NO

Publish a sincere response that addresses the issue. Apologize if an apology is due and focus on strengthening relationships with stakeholders. Continue to monitor the situation, responding when appropriate.

Monitor the situation. Prepare a sincere response that addresses the issue, apologize if an apology is due, and focus on strengthening relationships with stakeholders. If the situation begins to garner more attention, publish the response. Continue to monitor and, if need be, escalate to crisis team.

Publish a sin... that addres... corrects the n... and focuses o... relations... stakeholde... to monitor t... responding wh...

VISIT **MELISSAAGNES.COM/FLOWCHART** TO

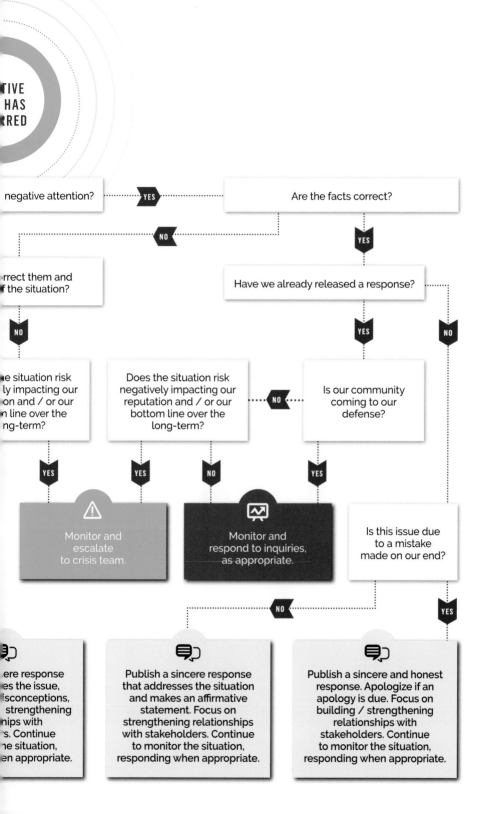

TIVE
HAS
RED

negative attention? **YES** Are the facts correct?

NO

rrect them and
f the situation? Have we already released a response?

NO **YES** **NO**

e situation risk
ly impacting our
on and / or our
n line over the
ng-term?

Does the situation risk
negatively impacting our
reputation and / or our
bottom line over the
long-term? **NO** Is our community
coming to our
defense?

YES **YES** **NO** **YES**

Monitor and
escalate
to crisis team.

Monitor and
respond to inquiries,
as appropriate.

Is this issue due
to a mistake
made on our end?

NO **YES**

ere response
es the issue,
sconceptions,
strengthening
nips with
s. Continue
e situation,
en appropriate.

Publish a sincere response
that addresses the situation
and makes an affirmative
statement. Focus on
strengthening relationships
with stakeholders. Continue
to monitor the situation,
responding when appropriate.

Publish a sincere and honest
response. Apologize if an
apology is due. Focus on
building / strengthening
relationships with
stakeholders. Continue
to monitor the situation,
responding when appropriate.

PRINT A FULL-SIZE COPY OF THIS FLOWCHART

In a crisis,

people expect the organization to hold itself accountable and responsible.

the power house at its Pensacola pulp and paper mill in Cantonment, Florida. No one at the mill was injured.

Response teams are working with local, state and federal agencies to provide information for those impacted. The incident released a mixture of wood fiber, water and pulping liquor into the surrounding community. We have engaged contractors to develop and implement plans to clean up and dispose of the discharged material as quickly as possible. We are providing all necessary support and resources to our local community and residents as we work through the clean-up. Our primary focus is on ensuring the health and safety of our employees, contractors and neighbors and on the clean-up of the affected areas and property.

Currently, the mill is not operating. We are assessing the extent of the damage to the mill, evaluating supply options and will be working closely with our customers to meet their needs.

Certain statements in this press release may be considered forward-looking statements. These statements reflect management's current views and are subject to risks and uncertainties that could cause actual results to differ materially from those expressed or implied in these statements. Factors which could cause actual results to differ include but are not limited to: (i) industry conditions, including but not limited to changes in the cost or availability of raw materials, energy and transportation costs, competition we face, cyclicality and changes in consumer preferences, demand and pricing for our products; (ii) global economic conditions and political changes, including but not limited to the impairment of financial institutions, changes in currency exchange rates, credit ratings issued by recognized credit rating organizations, the amount of our future pension funding obligation, changes in tax laws and pension and health care costs; (iii) unanticipated expenditures related to the cost of compliance with existing and new environmental and other governmental regulations and to actual or potential litigation; and (iv) whether we experience a material disruption at one of our other manufacturing facilities. These and other factors that could cause or contribute to actual results differing materially from such forward-looking statements are discussed in greater detail in the Company's Securities and Exchange Commission filings. We undertake no obligation to publicly update any forward-looking statements, whether as a result of new information, future events or otherwise."

While there's a lot that can be said about this statement, the aspect I want to draw your attention to is the last paragraph. Upon reading it, did anything strike you as being "off"? It's clear that IP's legal counsel wrote this paragraph, which makes up roughly 57% of the entire statement.

At a time when their community was dealing with black liquor-covered-everything, and was wondering whether this substance was toxic or presented consequences beyond just the mess it had made, IP released a communication that focused primarily on saving their own skins. How would this make you feel if you were worried about the air your children were breathing or the impact on your drinking water?

While it's important to manage the legal sides of crises, it's equally important to communicate with stakeholders using words that a) they comprehend, and b) appeal to them and the concerns they're experiencing. It is certainly important for your legal department to be a part of your crisis communications approval process, an aspect of your governance that we'll discuss in chapter four, but they should not *own* the process for drafting or strategizing your crisis communications.

Had IP released a more complete communication that met and addressed their stakeholders' expectations, demands, and

CRISIS READY RULE

A legal strategy is vital to dealing with a crisis, but it is *not* the public face of your response.

concerns, and had their legal department still insisted on a semblance of this disclaimer being included in the communication, they could have, for example, made it shorter and reduced the size of the font of the disclaimer. As it reads now, the impression it left with stakeholders was that the organization cared more about covering their own legal liability than the impact the explosion had on the community or the environment.

Caring people should write your crisis communications, not powerhouse attorneys.

7. IN A CRISIS, PEOPLE EXPECT ANSWERS TO THEIR MOST PERTINENT QUESTIONS

Marketing experts will tell you that when it comes to marketing, you want to focus on your audience's pain points and answer questions about how your product or service helps or benefits your clients or customers. Basically, you want to answer the question, "What's in it for me?" Similarly, in a crisis, your stakeholders will have pain points (I want to say "duh" here, but I won't. Or maybe I just did!), and they will expect you to address and answer the questions and concerns that directly apply to them. Additionally, each stakeholder group may have different concerns and questions, which is partly why identifying your stakeholder groups is so beneficial to your crisis preparedness.

The sooner you address and answer these questions, the better you will be able to get ahead of the noise and establish your organization as the controller of the crisis and its narrative.

For example, using the IP scenario we saw in the previous point, at the onset of this type of industrial accident crisis, which resulted in a black liquor release, we could expect that the affected community would care about receiving answers to the following types of questions:

- What is this substance and is it dangerous to our health or the environment?

- If it is dangerous, what precautions or actions do we need to take to avoid contamination / keep our families and ourselves safe and healthy?

- How long before it will be cleaned up?

- How is the organization going to help us clean, and compensate us for the damage it has caused to our property?

Meanwhile, IP's customers would want to know things like:

- How will this incident impact production of our goods and products?

- How long until operations resume at full capacity?

- How will the organization continue to meet our short-term needs while business is impacted?

These are all predictable and reasonable questions. The longer you take to give people the answers to their primary concerns, the more frustration and loss of trust you will experience against your organization. Thankfully, once you have identified your high-risk scenarios (which we will do together in chapter four), it's easy to determine what your stakeholders' most pertinent questions will be.

8. IN A CRISIS, PEOPLE EXPECT THE ORGANIZATION TO HOLD ITSELF ACCOUNTABLE AND RESPONSIBLE

When Wells Fargo was caught creating fake accounts on behalf of their nonconsenting customers in September of 2016, the organization tried everything in its power to get ahead of the story and mitigate the inevitable damaging impact.

For example, they put full-page ads in newspapers and used phrases like, "[we] take full responsibility" and "our commitment to you." They were proactive, timely, and loud in their crisis response. Yet, nothing worked. Why? Because, as this was a crisis that stemmed from the depths of the bank's culture, they were doing everything *except* holding their leadership truly accountable—which was the one gesture they needed to make in order to demonstrate that they were truly taking responsibility, righting wrongs, and committing to change.

Sure, John Stumpf, the bank's CEO at the time, told the House of Representatives Financial Services committee on September 29th, 2016, that he was "fully accountable for all unethical sales practices in our retail banking business". But the truth was that his actions didn't match his words; therefore, his words meant nothing. For example, as a crisis management tactic, the bank attempted to blame low-level employees and managers for incentivizing and condoning the scams that took place. It wasn't until Stumpf stepped down from his position as CEO and forfeited millions in pay that the real management of the crisis was able to begin. The bank had to take real responsibility for this cultural crisis, and hold itself accountable through its *actions.*

People—including customers, the general public, and lawmakers on Capitol Hill—demanded more of Wells Fargo. When the organization is at fault, the best crisis response in the world won't work until true responsibility and accountability is taken. People aren't fooled by meaningless words, no matter how good they may sound!

Getting back to Oscar Munoz's heart attack

At the start of this chapter, I asked you to jot down your initial thoughts regarding United Airline's response to Munoz's hospitalization. Now that we have thoroughly discussed the baseline expectations that your stakeholders will have of your organization in a crisis, let's use this knowledge to analyze the airline's response, and compare your initial observations with everything you now know.

United's statement said three things:

1. "Our CEO is in the hospital." It did not state why. By omitting this piece of information—information that was already being shared and reported about by the *WSJ* and other credible media sources—United sent the message that they were not being completely transparent with the information they had on-hand.

    Even if this detail had not already been a known fact, and let's say that United was not in a position to disclose the details regarding Munoz's medical condition (though a public company's CEO's health risks may be deemed financially material information that requires disclosure), they still could have, and should have, said more than they did.

    For example, they could have said something like, "We have been informed by Oscar's family that he was admitted to the hospital earlier today, and while it's too soon to know the details of his medical condition at this time, we are in regular communication with his family and will provide you with another update as soon as we receive more information."

This type of transparency would have come across as honest and shown a sincere willingness to communicate, even if their hands may have been tied—especially had they come out with it prior to the media reporting on the incident. It would have been much better than simply omitting or choosing to not address this relevant—and important—part of the story. It's never a good decision to blatantly avoid the elephant in the room. The elephant is big. Everybody sees it. It can't be avoided, and an attempt to avoid it will only negatively reflect upon your organization.

2. "We will update you as we deem it appropriate." United was already off to a bad start, weren't they? They only released this minimalist statement because the situation was garnering unwanted attention that was affecting stock price. In addition, in the same breath they chose to omit a piece of important information that was already circulating. These actions left their stakeholders wondering exactly when United would "deem it appropriate" to provide sufficient details. Due to their chosen timeline of response and the brevity of that response once it was finally released, stakeholders already distrusted United's capacity to provide them with updates that were relevant to them.

3. "We are continuing to operate normally." How so? Your CEO is in the hospital and, as a result, you canceled a scheduled labor summit with union leaders. How is this normal business operation? What is your plan to continue operating normally? Do you have a succession plan in place? If so, what is it and under what conditions will it be triggered? Do you see where I'm going with this? None of the pertinent—and predictable—questions were answered in any satsifactory way.

If we evaluate United's response with the eight expectations discussed in this chapter, let's look at how they fared:

- Prompt notification: **Fail**

- Transparency: **Fail**

- Timely, consistent communication: **Fail**

- Listen to and validate emotions: **Fail**

- Two-way communication: **Fail**

- Human tone, rather than corporate tone: **Fail**

- Answers to pertinent questions: **Fail**

- Responsibility and accountability taken: Luckily for United, this one doesn't apply in this situation.

So, how does this match up with what I asked you to write towards the beginning of this chapter? If you guessed along these lines, great! If not, then hopefully you learned a thing or two about the importance of your stakeholders' expectations, and how to go about meeting them in a way that fosters trust and credibility.

THE IMPACT OF FAILURE

When United issued this response to the situation, it unsurprisingly did nothing to subside their stakeholders' key concerns. As a result, over the weekend that followed, the media continued to criticize the organization's poor response. On top of that, social media continued to run rampant with speculation, wondering who would step in for Munoz as interim CEO.

It wasn't until United released a more thorough response to the situation the following Monday evening, one that confirmed facts and addressed and answered the pertinent questions on their key stakeholders' minds, that they began to see their stock price rise back up to normal levels, and the noise, speculation, and media reports subside.

> **United's CRP in this situation, which was 3% of its market capitalization within twenty-four hours, was due to both the organization's chosen timeline of response and its inadequacy of response. This CRP was entirely preventable.**

Taking the time to understand your stakeholders' expectations now, prior to a crisis, will give you key advantages at the onset of a crisis, and help you mitigate and prevent a lot of unnecessary backlash. Had United released a more thorough statement on the Thursday when Munoz was admitted to the hospital and the summit was postponed, or even on the Friday when the media began to report on the incident, the airline could have gotten ahead of the news and immediately addressed and calmed their stakeholders' concerns. Instead, they chose to suffer through continued blows that helped to chip away at their credibility and market trust.

All of this is in your power to do now, and is key. Key to both your day-to-day business opportunities—because understanding your stakeholders' expectations can only serve you well in all times, not just in times of crisis—

and key to your crisis management. Identify your stakeholder groups, seek to understand their expectations of your organization when times get tough, and put measures in place to enable your team to successfully meet those expectations in real time, every time. With the advantage this gives your organization you'd be foolish not to take these steps now, right? So then, what are you waiting for?

04

TO BE OR NOT TO BE (A CRISIS)?

Live, during the 2017 Academy Awards ceremony, *La La Land* was named the winner of the coveted Best Picture award. Minutes later, after *La La Land*'s cast and crew had already taken to the stage and were giving their acceptance speech, the film's producer, Jordan Horowitz, claimed the audience's attention by announcing that there had been a mistake. *La La Land* was not the winner, *Moonlight* was.

The world watched as confusion and embarrassment took place. Finally, *Moonlight* director Barry Jenkins took to the stage to claim the Oscar.

As can be expected, the world took notice and the incident immediately went viral. The media reported on the embarrassing moment, naming PricewaterhouseCoopers as the ones responsible for the mix-up, while social media exploded with commentary, reactions and discussions. For days, the buzz was all about the Oscars' crisis.

But was this *really* a crisis for the Oscars? The answer is no, it absolutely was not. A crisis for the Oscars would be, for example, something like a terrorist attack. What occurred on Sunday, February 26th, 2017, at the 89th Academy Awards ceremony, was an *issue* for the Oscars. A viral issue, but an issue nonetheless.

However, the same can't be said for PricewaterhouseCoopers (PwC) or its two partners responsible for the mishap. PwC is a multinational professional services firm that, since 1934,[21] has been responsible for tallying the Oscar votes, determining who won, and handing the presenters the envelopes that contain the names of the winners throughout the ceremony. Unlike for the Oscars, this mix-up was more than an issue for PwC and its two partners. It was the makings of a crisis.

Why? Let's examine. PwC leverages its long-standing relationship with the Academy as a way to highlight their trustworthiness and their dependability—both incredibly important aspects of an accounting firm. In a matter of seconds, their credibility and dependability was called into question, and millions of people were there to watch it happen live. If they did not manage this incident well, it could present a long-term negative impact on the organization's reputation.

As for the two partners responsible for the blunder, their professional reputations were put on the line that night, as was their physical safety when they began receiving death threats,[22] with pictures of their homes shared on social media.

Meanwhile, while the Academy was subjected to an incredibly embarrassing moment, the incident didn't threaten any long-term damage to their reputation in any way. This blunder wasn't their fault and therefore did not threaten to negatively reflect upon them. As a result, this was not a crisis for the Oscars. It was an embarrassing issue that needed to be managed in the heat of the moment. And it was.

It is important to understand that, just because something is a crisis for one organization, does not necessarily mean it is a crisis for another organization. It all depends on the incident's potential long-term impact on the organization, and different incidents impact different organizations in different ways.

This means that it is critical for your team to be able to clearly identify the difference between an issue and a crisis, in order for your organization to be able to respond effectively and appropriately to a negative situation. Using a fire extinguisher on an entire kitchen for a burned pop tart will create a ginormous, unnecessary mess. Over-reacting or under-reacting to an incident will do the same. Miscategorizing can make or break a situation.

ISSUE VS. CRISIS

One thing I've come to learn in my years of consulting is that far too often, professionals get confused by the difference between an issue and a crisis. This confusion itself is a risk.

While the confusion can be understandable, considering all the realities and challenges we face in both instances, to be crisis ready, your team needs to be able to instinctively identify the true potential impact of a given situation and take the appropriate steps to either respond or escalate it internally.

Fortunately, crises have some clear characteristics which, when you know what they are, you can frame as questions to help your team quickly assess the potential impact of a negative situation. So, to begin, let's define what a crisis is, and then frame it as a question for your team to use to help them properly assess a negative situation.

A crisis is:

a negative event or situation that impacts, or threatens to impact, people (stakeholders), the environment, business operations, the organization's reputation and / or the organization's bottom line, over the long-term. A crisis is a negative event that will stop business as usual to some extent, as it will require immediate attention and guidance from leadership.

An issue is:

a negative event or situation that either does not stop business as usual, and / or does not threaten long-term negative impact on any of the five business attributes listed above. However, this is not to say that issues aren't important to quickly detect and manage. Mismanaged issues can and do develop into crises.

Does the situation impact, or risk impacting:

- *People,*

- *The environment,*

- *Business operations,*

- *The organization's reputation, and / or*

- *The organization's bottom line...*

...over the <u>long-term</u>?

This is a powerful question that will help your team evaluate the incident through the right lens.

Let's Compare

To make this real, let's bring the Oscars example back and evaluate the incident's potential long-term impact for each of the three parties involved.

ACADEMY AWARDS

STOP BUSINESS AS USUAL?	No. It was a minor blip, and the show went on.
THREATEN LONG-TERM IMPACT?	This incident did not threaten long-term impact on: • the audience or members of the Academy, • the environment, • business operations, • the Academy's reputation, as they were not responsible for this blunder, • the Academy's bottom line.
ISSUE OR CRISIS?	Issue

PWC

STOP BUSINESS AS USUAL?	Yes. It was necessary for PwC to release a statement that acknowledged the mix-up and demonstrated that the situation was being taken seriously. Additionally, over the next few days, you can imagine what must have gone on within the organization: the right people needed to gather and figure out what they needed to do on their end to mitigate the potential long-term impact of the incident on the brand. For example, • They needed to initiate an investigation to determine the root cause of the mix-up; • They needed to speak with members of the Academy to address any loss of trust with their long-standing client; and • They needed to take appropriate action to reassure the Academy, and their other stakeholders, how they planned to prevent this situation from happening again.
THREATEN LONG-TERM IMPACT?	The incident, if not managed properly, threatened long-term negative impact on PwC's reputation and, therefore, potentially its bottom line.
ISSUE OR CRISIS?	Potential crisis

THE TWO PWC PARTNERS

STOP BUSINESS AS USUAL?	Absolutely. Right from the second they realized that they had handed off the wrong envelope, they were in crisis mode. They needed to stop everything and manage the situation.
THREATEN LONG-TERM IMPACT?	This incident threatened: • their professional reputations, • potentially their bottom line had they lost their positions at the firm, and • their physical safety (their persons).
ISSUE OR CRISIS?	Crisis

By arming your team with an understanding of the difference between an issue and a crisis, and by providing them with the definitions and question mentioned above, you will help them clearly and effectively identify rising risks.

Your Turn!

I like to make things real, and what better way to do this than by playing a little game? Earlier in the book, you learned of a number of different stories and case studies. Now it's time for you to determine whether the incidents are issues or crises for the organizations, and why.

Ready?

Here we go…

- Was the hashtag-gone-wrong-campaign that my client experienced, found in chapter one, an issue or a crisis for the city?

- Was the challenge that Emory University Hospital faced, found in chapter two, an issue or a crisis for the hospital?

- Was the incident that my client experienced, the one that left a foul smell lingering in the air, found in chapter two, an issue or a crisis for the organization?

- Did Oscar Munoz's heart attack, found in chapter two, present an issue or a crisis for United Airlines?

- Was the explosion that International Paper experienced, found in chapter two, an issue or a crisis for the organization?

- Was the Wells Fargo scandal, found in chapter three, an issue or a crisis for the bank?

ANSWERS: Issue; Issue; Issue (that unnecessarily escalated to the point of virality); Crisis; Crisis.

Play this type of game with your teams and help them hone their risk assessment skills. The goal is for your entire team to be able to instinctively spot a rising risk and determine whether it is an issue or a potential crisis for the organization. This plays a big role in being crisis ready.

BE CAREFUL WHAT YOU CALL THINGS

I've hinted at how much the term "social media crisis" annoys me, and it is finally time to address it! "Social media crisis" is a trendy term these days. But contrary to popular belief, there is no such thing. In fact, labeling a crisis as a "social media crisis" puts your organization at a disadvantage. Let me explain.

Let's use *United Breaks Guitars* as the crisis example here. *United Breaks Guitars* was a YouTube video sensation, created and published by Dave Carroll in 2009, that instantly went viral and garnered so much negative attention from the public on social media that it sent United's stock plummeting by 10%. The video is still viewed and referenced today in discussions about customer service and terrible issue management. Knowing what we know about the criteria of a crisis, this event was a crisis for the airline at the time.

However, while the crisis originated and escalated on social media, and therefore was labeled a social media crisis, the root cause of the crisis was certainly not social media. It was an operational issue that developed into a customer service issue and, ultimately, revealed a cultural crisis for the airline. (Interesting how eight years later, we're still presented with much ammunition for the argument that United has a cultural crisis. Hmmm.... But I digress. Or do I?)

By labeling a negative event as a social media crisis, you miss the opportunity to identify, and then fix, the deeper issue, because social media is never the true, underlying cause of a crisis. Additionally, as we saw in chapter two, social media is an unavoidable factor of all crises. This means that when a crisis strikes, no matter where or how it originates, it will have a presence, and may even escalate, on social media. So really, every crisis should be labeled a "social media crisis."

The reason I'm so adamant about not using the term "social media crisis" is that the term does little to really serve the organization. If your intent is to be truly crisis ready, then understanding the difference between an issue and a crisis is critical for your crisis prevention and crisis management. Most often, incidents that are labeled "social media crises" are nothing more than issues that have gone viral, or, as we just saw, the root cause of the crisis has far more to do with a bigger underlying issue, and therefore, blaming social media will not enable you to truly remedy the much bigger problem.

The term "social media crisis" is used by people who do not know the difference between issues and crises. And you are certainly not one of those people!

THE OPPORTUNITY IN ISSUES

Another reason why clearly understanding the difference between an issue and a crisis is so important is that, as I briefly mentioned earlier, a crisis will often develop due to a mismanaged issue. As a result, effective issue management is one of the secrets to successful crisis prevention and crisis management.

Furthermore, the way you manage an issue will do one of two things:

1. Each mismanaged issue will chip away at the trust and credibility, and therefore the reputation, of your organization; or

2. Each well-managed issue will present an opportunity to strengthen trust, credibility, and goodwill with your stakeholders.

Because issues are not crises (yet!), they present unique opportunities. Just as we saw with the city's hashtag campaign situation in chapter one, when you manage an issue well, not only will you mitigate its potential to escalate to crisis level, but you can use the opportunity to live the values

**CRISIS
READY RULE**

There is no such
thing as a social
media crisis!

of your organization, prioritize your stakeholder relationships, build trust, and make deposits into your bank of goodwill.

The more your team is capable of successfully managing the little bumps in the road that are inevitable in every business, the better versed they will be at meeting stakeholder expectations and making smart decisions when the bumps grow into high-impact mountains. Remember the crisis mindset we discussed in chapter one? Successfully managing real-time issues is a great time to reward the right mindset and further embed the right culture.

WHAT'S THE WORST THAT CAN HAPPEN?

Historically, a crisis management plan was a very thick binder that provided a roadmap for managing all types of crises. Today, crises escalate far too quickly, and there are far too many nuances in the different ways to respond and manage different crises. For this reason, I don't recommend taking a generalist approach to your crisis preparedness. This won't give you the best advantage at implementing a crisis ready culture.

Instead, the best way to be crisis ready is to identify your organization's high-risk scenarios and uniquely prepare for each one. This is precisely what we're going to do together over the next few chapters.

Every organization has a handful of high-risk scenarios that are the most likely types of high-impact crises to strike. Doesn't it make sense to identify them, prevent the preventable, and put your team in the best possible position to be prepared to successfully manage the unpreventable?

What if your organization identifies ten high-risk scenarios and wisely chooses to do a "deep-dive" into each one, and an eleventh scenario strikes? Because of all the work you will have done to understand, prepare, and train, your team will instinctively know what to do to manage the eleventh scenario. I'll say it again: instinctive successful crisis management is our ultimate goal here.

For this reason, while you may develop a crisis ready program based on your organization's high-risk scenarios, you also need to make sure that the program is scalable and adaptable. This will help your team be crisis ready for all types of negative events, and it will also help you develop a program that will grow and expand with the organization as it evolves over time. These are two very important features of a robust crisis ready program.

So, now that you're armed with an understanding of issues versus crises, let's take the next step, which is to identify your organization's high-risk scenarios.

Odds are, you probably already have a good idea of what your organization is vulnerable to. However, I'd bet money that you do not currently have the whole picture.

To begin identifying your high-risk scenarios, start by creating a list of what you believe to be your organization's most pertinent risks. You can then use this list as a starting point for discussion with your management team. And yes, your management team must absolutely be involved in this process.

As we discussed briefly in chapter two, identifying your high-risk scenarios needs to be a collaborative initiative—the reason being that each member of management has a different relationship with the brand, as well as a different area of expertise and focus. Therefore, while you may have certain high-risk scenarios that keep you up at night, they may have entirely different ones. It is only by identifying and discussing each of these scenarios that you will be in a position to build out a comprehensive list.

To help you guide this important discussion, following are some questions that will help you extract the information you're seeking during this process. Feel free to adapt and expand upon them as you see fit.

Questions for your high-risk scenario discussion:

- What risks or crisis scenarios do you believe to be the most likely to strike the organization?

- Are there industry-specific crisis scenarios that the organization is vulnerable to?

- What crises or potential crises has the organization experienced in the past that may resurface in the future, for whatever reason?

- What types of crises have competitors or colleagues experienced that could apply to the organization?

- What types of crises might our key stakeholders be vulnerable to, which, if they were to occur, risk directly or indirectly impacting the organization? For example, if a key service provider were hacked, and as a result, the hackers gained access to the organization's internal systems, would this present a potential crisis for the organization?

HOW MANY IS TOO MANY?

There is no right number of high-risk scenarios. There is only "your" number. That being said, if you identify fifty high-risk scenarios, you have far too many! The objective is to identify the most pertinent and high-impact types of *crises*—not issues—that might strike your organization. In my experience, a typical organization has a range of anywhere between five and twelve high-risk scenarios. If you've identified more than that, then they can probably be better categorized.

For example, I once had a client identify "a disgruntled employee being a bad actor" and "allegations of business-related misconduct against an employee" as two different scenarios. When I asked them to provide me with specific examples that would better help me understand each scenario and their thought process behind them, we quickly realized that these were one in the same scenario. We simply needed to rework the title of the scenario, which became "allegations of misconduct against an employee in the workplace."

Furthermore, you may experience a situation that ends up being a combination of two different high-risk scenarios. This is okay and completely plausible. For example, what if heavy machinery was hacked by a malicious outside party and used to wreak havoc at one of your business's sites of operation, resulting in significant business disruption and possibly even harming people in the process? This crisis could be a combination of a cybersecurity incident and an onsite accident or catastrophe.

In developing your program, each of these high-risk scenarios should be identified, explored, and prepared for individually, as this will give you the most comprehensive understanding of, and preparation for, the crisis. However, when managing this crisis, your team would use a combination of each of these scenario's playbooks and handbooks (more on these two resources later), to help guide your decisions, actions and communications throughout the management of the incident.

With all of that said, some common high-risk scenarios to help you get started are listed below. Which ones apply to your organization will depend on the nature of your business. Remember that when identifying your high-risk scenarios, think only in terms of crisis-level incidents, not issues. To remain focused on identifying crises, ask the team, "at what point would this scenario become a crisis and why?" Then write down some scenario examples to help make the scenarios real, and to make sure everybody is on the same page.

- Cybersecurity incident
- Executive or employee misconduct in the workplace
- Executive or employee misconduct outside the workplace, with direct impact on the organization
- Foodborne illness / contamination
- Key person event*
- Misconduct or failure of a key external stakeholder that directly impacts the organization
- Misstatement of financials

- Natural disaster
- Offsite accident or catastrophe
- Onsite accident or catastrophe
- Organized activism against the organization
- Product failure
- Regulatory incident
- Workplace disruption
- Workplace violence

*An executive or high-profile team member's death, incapacitation, disappearance, kidnapping, etc.

I recommend ranking your high-risk scenarios, to the greatest extent possible, in order of likeliness to occur. This will be the order in which you conduct your deep-dives while developing your crisis ready program.

For Example

Pretend your organization is a restaurant with one or multiple locations. Following are some of the high-risk scenarios that should absolutely be on your list:

Cybersecurity incident

e.g.: Your organization is the victim of a malicious hack, whereby millions of your customers' personally identifying and financial information has been breached.

Foodborne illness / contamination

e.g.: E. coli is discovered in one of your ingredients and people in multiple regions and locations have fallen ill. Some have been hospitalized and two senior citizens have died as a direct result. You aren't sure where the E. coli originated from, or how far the contamination has been spread.

Executive or employee misconduct in the workplace

e.g.: A group of employees reveal, by means of a viral YouTube video, that they have been contaminating the food for months. The video is highly explicit and revolting.

Misconduct or failure of a key external stakeholder that directly impacts the organization

e.g.: It is revealed that one of your biggest and most public suppliers / partners has been unethical with their produce. A public investigation ensues and the supplier is launched into a viral crisis, with your organization being caught in the middle.

Natural disaster

e.g.: A natural disaster demolishes one or several of your most profitable locations, rendering them inoperable for months.

Workplace violence

e.g.: A tragic mass shooting occurs at one of your restaurants by an angry past employee, killing and injuring customers and employees.

Once this list is drafted, circulate it with an extended group of people within the organization to gain consensus. The more input and contemplation you request and receive the more comprehensive your understanding of your organization's most pertinent risks will be, and the more you will begin to subconsciously get the team prepared for the upcoming development and integration of your crisis ready program.

As you know, time is of the essence in a crisis, so the more thorough you are in your prep work, the better prepared for real-time crisis management your team will be. Additionally, you'll learn that through this deep-dive process you will naturally end up revealing underlying elements that will offer advantages to the organization that far exceed just crisis management and preparedness. This happens every time I help a client develop their crisis ready program, which is part of the reason why I believe so passionately in this process.

So, with all of this said, what are your organization's high-risk scenarios, in ranked order?

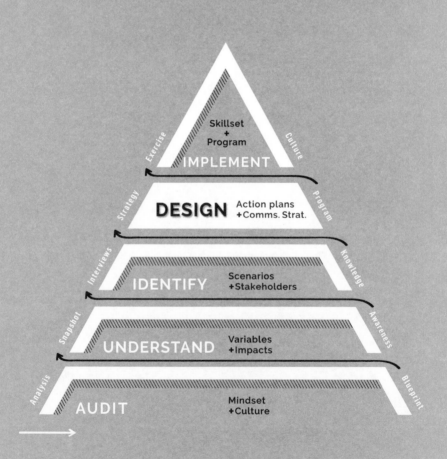

05

GETTING READY, READY, READY!

One of the only things that you can count on in a crisis is that situations are unpredictable. Crises unfold in unexpected ways, and even the best-laid plans can be jumbled up by unexpected twists and turns. What better exemplifies this characteristic of a crisis than a wildfire? Yes, meteorologists can usually predict all sorts of weather conditions...humidity, wind speed and direction, and so on. Having a good handle on these things can certainly go a long way towards managing a wildfire. However, even with all the tools and technology we have at our disposal, we cannot ever know *exactly* what the wind is going to do. It can change direction and, therefore, change the direction of the crisis management strategy without notice.

The point is that circumstances can never be completely predetermined. When a crisis strikes, members of your trained crisis team may be missing or unreachable, which means that your team has to scramble to do the work of many with just a few. There are many unpredictable events that can occur from minute to minute, and certain things are simply outside both our control and the analytic ability of our predictive models. This means that, while planning and exercises are a big part of building a crisis ready culture, so must be an ability to be versatile, flexible, and adaptable.

In May 2016, the Horse River Wildfire hit Fort McMurray, the urban center of the Regional Municipality of Wood Buffalo in Alberta, Canada, and approximately 88,000 people had to be evacuated from their homes in the span of a few hours. The majority of the 88,000 evacuees were unable to return to their homes for almost one month, with many unable to return until four months later. The impact of the wildfire was unprecedented in Canada's history, and had an economic impact that was large enough to directly affect Canada's GDP.

This catastrophic event threatened the immediate safety of the community, and ended up destroying 2,579 homes. Imagine the weight of responsibility resting on the shoulders of the task forces and emergency managers responsible for conducting the evacuation.

One of those responsible parties was Jordan Redshaw. When I spoke with Jordan, the communications manager with the recovery task force at the Regional Municipality of Wood Buffalo, he explained that Fort McMurray is a community that needs to be—and is— very crisis ready, as they are located in a region that naturally lives with many threats. High-risk scenarios, from floods to wildfires, are always demanding proper preparation from the community.

Learn more about the crisis management tactics Jordan and his team leveraged in this crisis: melissaagnes.com/ fortmcmurray

During these particular wildfires in 2016, the fire cut off road access to the Emergency Operating Center (EOC) where Jordan and his colleague, Robin Smith, were responsible for communicating with the community, providing them the information they needed to safely evacuate the area. As a result, Jordan and Robin were the only two people performing this critical task of communication for the initial hours of the evacuation.

This meant that two people needed to quickly and effectively manage media interviews, monitor and triage inquiries, develop messaging, and have it approved and disseminated through the right channels...all in a situation where doing this effectively could literally mean the difference between life and death. After hearing Jordan recount his experience and the team's challenges, it didn't come as a surprise when Jordan told me that the most important lessons he learned from managing this crisis was that, even with all their training and planning, the biggest advantages he and Robin had were their ability to quickly adjust their tactics to meet their objectives, and having immediate access to senior leaders. He explained that the rate of change they faced was so intense that one of the keys to their success was the ability to put themselves in the right state of mind to accept unpredictability, and be nimble enough to rapidly adapt and change with the circumstances.

PLAN VS. PROGRAM

Have you noticed that I keep referring to your crisis preparedness as a *program*, rather than a crisis management *plan?* This isn't coincidence. It is intended and there is a good reason. When you think of a plan, what do you think about? Most people think of a linear approach to a situation...a specific, unidirectional plan that says if A happens, they will do B. Let's think of your plan to get out of a burning building. You probably have an exit route in mind and your plan is to *get out* and get to safety as quickly as possible. That's a good plan, but it's linear. It doesn't prepare you for unforeseeable obstacles that may occur. For example, what if the exit door you have in mind is obstructed by fire or burning debris? What if the fire breaks out and you are in an unfamiliar part of the building? Do you know where all the nearest exits are, depending on where you are and what your circumstances may be?

Do you see where I am going with this? Crisis management isn't a linear strategy. Unforeseeable, unexpected developments *will* occur, sometimes amplifying the challenges, and other times lightening the load. This is why I always stress that you want to get your team to a level of preparedness that is instinctive, rather than solely being dependent on a linear plan that cannot possibly account for all the variations, bumps, and turns that may present themselves. A plan, in and of itself, tends to be very linear; crisis management is everything but.

I'll never forget the time I heard a client yell to her team member, "Throw that damn book away! It's inhibiting us!" You see, we had been conducting a very intense crisis simulation, and my client was correct. Her team kept relying solely on the plan, frantically searching through the hundreds of pages, expecting it to have all the answers to the curveballs the simulation was presenting. There was no way that the plan could incorporate everything, and it was affecting the team's ability to think creatively and be adaptive in a way that would help them overcome the challenges in front of them.

Now, I'm clearly not suggesting that a crisis management plan is useless. In fact, the act of planning is an invaluable, required exercise when implementing a crisis ready culture. However, the decision to rely solely on a crisis plan will put you at a disadvantage. The goal is to get to a place where the plan acts as an important crisis management resource that is there to be referenced when needed, but that your team is not entirely dependent on to successfully manage a crisis.

This is where the *program* aspect comes into play. Instead of solely developing a crisis management plan, over the next few chapters we are going to develop and implement a crisis ready program that will empower your team to be versatile and flexible, in order to manage any unforeseen obstacles that may come your way in the event of a crisis.

I'm not going to lie, it's going to take work. However, you have come this far, so you have everything it takes and I'll be with you every step of the way. Are you ready? Because the fun is about to begin!

As you navigate through the following chapters of this book, I encourage you to take the time to read each section, even if you feel you already have a particular element of your crisis preparedness "down." For example, you may already have a crisis management governance structure, so you may feel inclined to skip that part. Even if that's the case, I encourage you to read that section anyway, and use it to either validate or help you strengthen what you already have. We can call this choice being "crisis smart" ;-)

STRUCTURING YOUR PROGRAM

To give you an idea of what you are about to create, your comprehensive crisis ready program will be broken down into the following, each of which we will develop together over the next few chapters.

The foundation of your program

This is where you bring crisis readiness to every process, protocol, and structure that already exists within your organization, strengthening them as you evaluate them through the crisis ready lens.

While the foundation of the program will be created into a document, it is important to note that this document is not to be used in the midst of a breaking crisis. Instead, it will serve for training purposes, and as a reference for implementing crisis management best practices. Each of its components need to be internalized long before a crisis strikes, by every member of your organization.

The scenario-specific playbooks and handbooks

This is where your high-risk scenarios come into play. This is also the part of your crisis ready program that is meant to serve as that in-crisis "resource" I mentioned above. These resources will be designed with the first twenty-four to forty-eight hours of a breaking crisis in mind. As a result, they need to be extremely practical. Each scenario will have a playbook that houses your behind-the-scenes crisis management action plans, as well as a crisis communication handbook, which will detail your crisis communication strategies, and your pre-drafted, pre-approved crisis communications.

Another way to look at these elements is that the foundation of the program is a company-wide philosophy of crisis management, while the playbooks and handbooks house strategies and resources for specific crisis scenarios.

WHERE TO BEGIN

While the foundation of the program is the first place to begin—you can't develop a playbook without knowing your crisis management governance structure, for example—in my experience the most efficient way to tackle this process is to begin with developing the program's foundation *and* the creation of your first high-risk scenario playbook simultaneously.

Approaching the process in this way helps make it tangible. This enables you to develop protocols that are practical and effective, as you will have an actual scenario in mind to think through and discuss with team members. From there, you will continue to strengthen the program as you dive into each subsequent high-risk scenario.

Fair warning: developing a program of this nature is hard work (though not as much hard work as the alternative!). Following is how we're going to tackle this work together:

- Chapter 5: Developing the foundation of your program

- Chapter 6: Developing your crisis management playbook

- Chapter 7: Developing your crisis communication handbook

So, let's begin, shall we?

COLLECTING THE DATA

If you have done the exercises outlined in the previous chapters, you are already equipped with more crisis preparedness information than most organizations out there. But you certainly don't have all the pieces of the puzzle. It is time to start collecting those remaining pieces. The best way to do this is to have discussions with the right people within your organization. This means that your next task is to:

- Identify who those people are;

- Prepare for these discussions; and

- Get on their calendars.

So, who should you speak with? Since the goal is to get a full picture of the puzzle, you will want to speak with every person who will play a role in your organization's crisis management. This means you should plan to get a hold of:

- Members of your leadership team

- Department heads

- Regional / divisional heads

- Stakeholder owners

- People who may have insights and answers regarding your first high-risk scenario

- Anyone else you feel is important to gain perspective from

Each of these groups has a different relationship with the brand and its stakeholders, which means that each of them can provide you with unique feedback and insights that will be invaluable towards developing a well-rounded and practical crisis ready program. Take a moment to draw up a list of these people. In creating this list, it will be helpful to consult your stakeholder list from chapter three, as well as your organizational structure, which will give you a visual of the organization's departments, regions and divisions. Go ahead. I have nowhere else to go, I'll wait.

Great! Now that you have your list, it is time to prepare your line of questioning. The more angles you cover and the more thorough you are when digging for answers, the more comprehensive your program will be. There is no such thing as a stupid question during this process.

The focus of these discussions will be on better understanding your organization's different teams, their functions and processes—along with their mindset regarding crisis preparedness and management—and any areas of strength and vulnerability that you can leverage, build upon, and improve throughout this process.

Below, I have listed a baseline of subjects that you should explore in these interviews. When I begin working with a new client, I use this list as a framework. I then build upon and customize this framework, focusing on adapting the questions to fit the client's industry, needs, and goals, along with each individual high-risk scenario. After all, no two companies are going to have the same market presence, goals, staff constitution, or level of existing crisis preparedness. There will be plenty of customization in this stage.

It is worth reiterating the importance of not assuming you already know the answers to any of your questions, at any time. Instead, start with a hypothesis, and take the time to prove yourself right or wrong. When I conduct this line of interviews with my clients, even if I've been given the same answer to the same question by the last five people I've interviewed, I don't assume that the next five will continue to give me that same answer. Sometimes I get a different answer, which gives me another— and sometimes unexpected—piece of the puzzle. After all, people interpret questions differently and you never know when you will be bowled over by a fresh and helpful perspective.

Functionality

These questions establish who does what, and how that affects team members' placement in the crisis management governance structure. If you aren't sure about someone's role, now is the time to ask! Examples of this line of questioning include:

- What is your role / function within the organization? (not pertaining to crisis management)

- Who do you / does your department report to?

- Which departments do you communicate / work with throughout your daily activities? What is the purpose of those communications?

- In the event of a crisis, what do you foresee your crisis management roles and responsibilities being?

- What would be the roles and responsibilities of your department / your team?

- Do you foresee any challenges in undertaking these roles, and if so, what is required to help you overcome these challenges?

Stakeholders

When considering stakeholders, you want to ensure that you understand which department is responsible for which stakeholder group, both internal and external. You also want to better understand how each department communicates with their stakeholders during their day-to-day activities, as well as what your interviewee perceives to be their stakeholders' crisis management expectations in the organization. If you need a refresher on identifying and incorporating stakeholders, refer to chapter three. Examples of this line of questioning can include:

- Which stakeholder relationships do you / does your department "own"?

- How do you communicate with these stakeholders in your day-to-day activities (e.g., email, phone calls, in-person, digitally, etc.)?

- In the event of a crisis, what do you believe your stakeholders would expect from your team / the organization?

- Do you currently feel confident that your department / team would be able to meet these expectations? If yes, how so? If no, please explain why not.

- In the event of [insert high-risk scenario], what would be the most pertinent questions that your stakeholders would expect answers to?

Honest review

Your aim here is to gain a clear perspective of the organization's strengths and weaknesses, from the perspective of each interviewee. This enables you to determine common aspects, as well as department- or region-specific aspects that should be addressed within this process. Some lines of questioning you may want to include here are:

- How prepared do you feel the organization currently is to manage a real-time crisis? Feel free to make this question real by providing the interviewee with a list of your identified high-risk scenarios.

- Which aspects of crisis management do you feel the organization and / or your team would excel at? Why?

- Which aspects of crisis management do you feel need improvement?

- Do you have any specific concerns that we can help you address / remedy throughout this process of developing the organization's crisis ready program?

Efficiency of communication

We addressed stakeholder expectations and practical means of communication above. Here, we want to establish the realistic obstacles and challenges each department anticipates…whether real or perceived. The answers will help you better understand their everyday processes and any barriers that may present themselves during a breaking crisis, such as time delays, personality conflicts, etc. Some discussion-guiding questions can include:

- What do you expect the process of drafting and disseminating the crisis communications for your key stakeholders to be?

- What does your current communications approval process look like?

- How long do you feel it would realistically take the organization to respond to an incident in the event of a crisis?

Defining success

Understanding how each interviewee defines successful crisis management will help you gain insight into their mindset, and help you develop a benchmark to measure the organization's success in each high-risk scenario. This question is straightforward:

- In the event of [insert high-risk scenario], what would successful crisis management look like?

These are general questions for each interviewee, designed to provide you with a global perspective of your organization's current processes and realities. Additionally, you want to think through some key functions and department-specific questions that apply to crisis management in general, as well as to each of your high-risk scenarios. This means designing a specific line of questioning targeted towards each department and function, including your communications department, compliance department, legal department, marketing department, media relations department, etc. For example, here are some samples of department-specific questions you'll want to ask and discuss:

Communications department:

- What is your process for drafting different types of communications for the organization?

- What communications are you responsible for drafting for the organization?

- What is your current process for disseminating those communications to the organization's different departments and team members?

- What does your approval process look like?

- Will each of these processes be practical in the event of a crisis? What challenges or bottlenecks may they present?

Compliance / legal departments:

- What are the legal / regulatory risks that we need to be aware of, in the event of [insert high-risk scenario]?

- How can we help your team mitigate / prevent / prepare for these risks?

- Are there any legal / regulatory restrictions that may inhibit, or present challenges to, our crisis management?

- If so, how can we prepare for, or plan to mitigate, these challenges?

Marketing department:

- How do you currently monitor social media?

- If an incident were to become public, how quickly would the organization learn about it?

- What are the organization's social media policies and guidelines?

- Is the social media team trained in issue management?

- What is the current internal escalation protocol when a negative event is flagged as being a severe issue or a potential crisis?

- Does your department / team have open communication with the organization's media relations team? How, when, and why—or why not—do you communicate?

Media relations department:

- Who is responsible for responding to media inquiries?

- Does every employee know where to refer incoming media inquiries?

- Does your department / team have open communication with the organization's communications / social media teams? How, when, and why—or why not—do you communicate?

Having these discussions helps you gain a comprehensive understanding of your organization's current level of preparedness, as well as each department's daily processes. They also enable you to better understand, develop, and strengthen the needed procedures for different aspects of your crisis management. Furthermore, they offer insight into the attitude of all those who will partake in some form of crisis management activity. Finally, they help you identify what is required to develop and implement a practical and scalable crisis ready program.

I often find that organizations' crisis management plans are developed in a very siloed manner, where a specific department (or the leadership team) undertakes the initiative on its own, isolated from the rest of the organization. This results in a less than practical plan. Successful crisis management requires cross-departmental collaborative action, so how can it be practical to approach crisis preparedness in a siloed fashion? It can't; it isn't. It is far better to develop a program that permeates the culture of the *whole* organization. A holistic approach that incorporates each relevant department will give your program more legs to stand on. Most importantly, this initiative is stronger because it is designed to be collaborative.

Once you have collected the data, you are ready to begin developing the foundation of your program. Your first step is to develop a practical crisis management governance model. After all, you need to know who is going to be a part of the crisis management team before you can start assigning their roles and responsibilities. Better to figure this out now than when everyone is reaching for the same fire extinguisher in confusion! So, let's do this.

CRISIS MANAGEMENT GOVERNANCE

A crisis management governance model dictates who within an organization makes up the crisis management team. This is the team responsible for the organization's crisis management and response. Governance models define everything from the structure, roles, and responsibilities of a crisis management team, straight through to the internal escalation processes.

There are three critical attributes of a strong crisis management governance structure that I want you to keep in mind moving forward. These three attributes are:

Alignment with the governance structure of your organization

It is important for your crisis management governance to be a natural and fluent fit for the organization. I have seen consultants try to use fancy terms when helping an organization develop its governance model. For example, some folks throw around terms like "Crisis Leadership Team," "Crisis Action Team," "Regional Crisis Management Team," or "Global Crisis Management Team." On top of this, they tend to use acronyms throughout the plan, which just makes it all that much more confusing! No one wants to have to figure out who the RCMT is, and how to contact them, as a crisis is unfolding.

Taking this approach, in my experience, is neither practical nor ideal. In fact, the last thing you want to be doing in a crisis is using terminology that isn't natural to the organization, and that people may not understand or may be confused by in the heat of the moment.

Instead, your crisis management governance should reflect the organizational structure with which all employees and team members are already familiar. This applies to everything from the decision-making and approval processes, to the language you choose to use.

Ensure each stakeholder group has a representative at the table

When assessing the scope and impact of an incident on your organization, you want to ensure that each stakeholder group, along with every potential business impact, has a place at the table to be considered and assessed. The way to ensure this is to have a well-rounded crisis management team.

For example, one of the most common and frequent frustrations I hear from HR departments is that employee communication is often an afterthought in times of issue or crisis management. Yet, employees are one of your key stakeholder groups and poor communication with them throughout the management of a crisis is detrimental to your crisis management success. The best way to avoid making this dire (yet common) mistake is to ensure your employees are represented; have HR be a part of the organization's crisis management team and you will be good to go.

Responsible vs. Accountable

These are two important distinctions. Everybody within your crisis management team will have specific roles and actions they will be responsible for implementing or overseeing. However, only a select few will actually be *accountable* for the organization's overall crisis management. This accountability falls on the shoulders of your leadership team. They are the decision-makers, and ultimately bear the weight of the organization's crisis management. Accountability can be delegated to one person, such as your CEO, or a collective few members of the c-suite. The answer depends on the current structure of your organization.

For example, take the case of Wells Fargo discussed briefly in chapter three. No matter what the bank did to try to manage their crisis, nothing worked until the CEO was truly held *accountable* and lost his job. As another example, in 2017, over a year after the Volkswagen scandal was discovered, six of the car manufacturer's executives were criminally charged[23] for their role in the crimes committed during the emission scandal. These six executives were held *accountable* for their part in committing these crimes.

Identifying and understanding who is accountable versus who is merely responsible for the organization's crisis management will help guide the right actions in the heat of the moment. By the way, had the CEO of Wells Fargo known that he was going to lose his position and his reputation, and had the six Volkswagen executives known they were going to face criminal charges, maybe both organizations would have been smarter in preventing and managing their respective crises. A thought worth considering, if you ask me.

WHO DOES WHAT?

Whom should you include within your crisis management governance? As a high-level overview, there should typically be three main groups within your governance model. While this structure may vary from organization to organization, using this approach as a starting point will help you fit this model to your organizational structure and needs. It is also worth noting that the names of these three groups are descriptive for this book; they are not the actual names you should use within your organization! These three groups are:

- The leadership team

- The responsible team

- The scenario-specific assessment groups

Who's in charge?

The leadership team will be comprised of the top members of your organization's leadership. No surprise there. They are the people responsible for declaring a corporate crisis, for making the tough decisions throughout the management of the crisis, and finally, they are—or at least some of them will be—accountable for the organization's crisis, as well as its management and response. Some crisis management responsibilities of this group include:

- Assessing the scope and potential impacts of the incident on the organization and its stakeholders.

- Declaring a corporate crisis and activating the appropriate crisis management teams and playbook(s).

- Deciding on the organization's crisis management strategy and response.

- Approving crisis communications in a timely fashion.

CRISIS READY RULE

No matter what happens to the ship, the captain is always responsible.

This team should be as small as possible, though it should also mirror the natural governance structure of your organization. I've worked with organizations whose leadership team naturally consisted of a handful of executives. The way these organizations' governance was structured meant that this group needed to make key decisions in concert, so it was only natural that their crisis management governance work the same way. On the other hand, I've also worked with organizations whose CEO was the ultimate decision maker. Therefore, these organizations' crisis leadership mirrored their natural governance structure.

Who gets it done?

The responsible team will include all those who are responsible for overseeing specific tasks and actions in the event of a crisis. Each department will have a role and responsibility in the event of a crisis, and each department and / or regional head will be responsible for delegating and overseeing those tasks. Therefore, each department head, regional head, divisional head, and / or stakeholder owner should be a part of this team. The members of this team will have some common roles and responsibilities, as well as unique department-specific roles and responsibilities. Every member will be responsible for things like:

- Advising the leadership team on their respective areas of expertise. For example, the head of your investor relations department will be responsible for assessing and advising leadership on the potential impacts on, as well as the expectations of, investors and the market.

- Carrying out the actions within their respective action plans.

- Ensuring prompt and effective communication with their respective stakeholders.

- Ensuring timely updates to the leadership team for the duration of the crisis.

Whereas department-specific roles and responsibilities will include things like:

- The communications department will be responsible for drafting the organization's crisis communications, ensuring prompt approval by the appropriate members of the leadership team, and quickly disseminating the communications to each department and stakeholder owner.

- The legal department will be responsible for overseeing and managing any legal risks throughout the management of the crisis.

- The compliance department will be responsible for ensuring the organization remains compliant with any industry and / or organizational regulations that may apply.

It is important to note that, depending on the size and structure of your organization, there may be overlaps within the leadership and action teams. However, it is still important to call them out, as one group is part of the decision-making process, while the other simply has responsibilities to execute.

Who assesses and escalates?

Your scenario-specific assessment groups are responsible for assessing the initial potential impact of a given situation, and determining whether it needs to be escalated to the crisis management team, i.e., the responsible and leadership teams. Depending on the identified risk, different people may be needed for this role, which is why these groups should be scenario-specific.

For example, consider again a cybersecurity crisis. In such a crisis, your IT team may be the first to detect the incident. But upon initial assessment, they aren't the right group, in and of themselves, to determine whether the incident constitutes a corporate crisis. They can only see the situation through their lens, which does not provide the full scope on potential impact to the organization. Therefore, you want to make sure to have a subset group of internal experts that the IT team knows to call in, to help them assess the potential scope and breadth of the situation and decide whether escalation is necessary. For a cybersecurity crisis, this group may include someone from your legal department, your compliance department, your risk management department, and any other department that the situation impacts.

The goal here is to have a group of qualified individuals that will quickly gather to determine whether the incident needs escalation. You want to ensure prompt escalation in the event of a potential crisis while also ensuring that you do not call leadership out of their busy schedules when a situation does not merit their attention. Not every situation is black and white. You need to account for many potential gray zones, and this is the group responsible for assessing them.

Roles and responsibilities of this group include:

* Quickly gathering with the appropriate members of this team.

* Assessing the initial scope and potential impact of a given incident.

* Determining whether the incident needs to be escalated, and to whom.

It's likely that these assessment groups already exist in your organization in an informal capacity, and it's your job to identify and strengthen the processes that are already at work. For example, when discussing the high-risk scenario of a cybersecurity crisis with your IT team, you may determine that they already have a group of specific people they call on when assessing the severity of a threat. This group may be exactly who is required; you just may need to formalize the process. It's all about asking the right questions and identifying the most practical processes and approaches for your crisis preparedness.

Who takes the lead?

For each of your high-risk scenarios, name one key person as the lead for managing the crisis. This lead will be the owner of the scenario's playbook, as they will have the biggest expertise in accordance with the scenario. For example, in the event of a cybersecurity crisis, the lead will be your chief information officer, whereas in the event of a regulatory crisis, the lead will be either your chief compliance or chief legal officer.

TAKING A LONG-TERM VIEW

I've mentioned throughout this book that one of our objectives is to develop a crisis ready program that will be applicable to all types of crises and issues. This program should be flexible enough to grow and evolve with your organization over time, but sturdy enough to hold up in the event of application. Developing a strong and robust governance structure is the first step in helping you achieve this. There are a few things you should keep in mind on this topic before we close out this chapter.

Firstly, your governance structure should be designed with *roles* and *functions* in mind, rather than specific people. For example, the chief operating officer will be a part of your crisis management team, and their role and responsibilities within the organization's crisis management need to depend on their area of expertise, *not* their personal characteristics, traits, qualities, and strengths. This is important, because while the roles and responsibilities assigned with that title will not change if there is a change in personnel, the characteristics of the person will. Then what? If you focus on people rather than function, each time there is a change in personnel you will have to redesign your entire governance structure.

Additionally, members of the crisis management team must be familiar with not just their roles and responsibilities, but the roles and responsibilities of each of their counterparts. Crises occur at inopportune times and can be extremely messy. People go on holiday, or might be otherwise unreachable in the event of a crisis. These things happen, and we all need a vacation every now and then! Even if you find yourself missing some team members, the incident will still need management, and the hope is that team members that *are* available can put on multiple hats to get the job done effectively. This also speaks to the importance of full-team trainings and ensuring each member of your crisis team has an alternate representative, or two—and that those alternates have proper training as well.

WHAT'S IN A NAME?

Every aspect of your crisis ready program needs to be practical, and mirror your organization's day-to-day language and processes. This applies to everything from the names you give your crisis management teams, to your internal escalation processes, approval processes, communication dissemination processes, and everything in between.

So, while I've used language like "leadership team" and "responsible team" above, these titles were used with generality in mind. If your organization naturally refers to its leadership team as "senior management" or "the managing committee," and the same people who comprise those groups belong to your crisis management leadership team as described above, then that is what you should call that team.

If, in the heat of the moment, you call out, "Where's the crisis responsible team?" there's a good chance that people will stare blankly at you and rack their brains trying to remember who that is. However, if your responsible team is made up of your department heads, and "department heads" is the term used to refer to this group of people on a daily basis, calling out, "Where are the department heads?" will get immediate recognition and response.

If you are doing your job properly, crises will be rare. And even though you're going to rehearse your program, keep it current, and put your staff through crisis team trainings (as we'll explore in chapter nine), the language and protocols you develop for your program need to represent the culture and daily habits of your day-to-day processes.

Try not to be hung up on fancy and confusing terminology. Make every component of your crisis ready program fit the natural culture and daily habits of your organization and its team members—though do strengthen these processes, as needed, throughout the development of your program. You will thank me for it in the heat of the moment.

FOUNDATIONAL ELEMENTS

After designing your governance structure, there are a few remaining elements required to finish developing the foundation of your program. Here, you will include the fundamental elements of your program that will not be included within your playbooks. While they are important from a structural purpose, they are not resources for your in-the-moment crisis management.

Following are some of the remaining foundational elements, shaped as questions, to answer and include as part of the foundation of your program:

- How does the organization define a crisis?

- What is the process for declaring a corporate crisis?

- How does the crisis ready program get activated?

- How and where is the program to be stored for quick and easy access?

- Where / how does the crisis management team meet during work hours, and during non-work hours, once the program is activated?

- Where is appropriate contact information stored?

- What are the organization's crisis management principles and guidelines?

- What are the crisis communication dissemination processes, for both internal and external dissemination? (More on this in chapter seven.)

- What is the process for maintaining the crisis ready program to ensure it is always kept current?

- What is the timeline and requirement for regular crisis team trainings?

These are all questions that need to be answered, if you're going to develop a crisis ready program that is meant to serve the organization over the long term. After developing the foundation of your program, it is time to develop your scenario-specific playbooks. When you're ready, I'll meet you over in chapter six!

06

ACTING ON PURPOSEFUL PURPOSE

Earlier, I mentioned the crisis that Domino's Pizza faced back in 2009—the one where two rogue employees at a Conover, NC restaurant recorded themselves doing disgusting things to food before it went out on delivery. When this crisis struck, Domino's corporate office did everything correctly behind the scenes. For example, they immediately closed the restaurant where the incident took place and had it completely sanitized; they fired and filed charges against the two employees responsible for the vile acts; they launched an investigation into whether or not the tampered food was actually delivered to customers; and they made sure this was an isolated event. They also strengthened their hiring policies and put measures in place to prevent, to the greatest extent possible, this type of behavior from happening again.[24]

However, what Domino's failed to do was communicate these actions to their concerned stakeholders. While the organization immediately took the right steps to manage the crisis, it took the brand two days to communicate their response[25] to the rest of the world. So, even though they were on top of their game taking action, the world had no idea they were doing these things because communication was poor. This mistake led to the brand experiencing some otherwise avoidable long-term impacts.

Because they were quiet for so long, the story continued to escalate and gain traction, giving customers the perception that Domino's did not care. While we now know this was *not* the case, perception is reality. Domino's lack of a timely, transparent, and compassionate response meant the incident had a more lasting effect on the brand than necessary. The restaurant branch where the incident occurred ended up closing its doors for good, and the brand's sales dropped two percent nationwide. Such dire repercussions were avoidable, had the organization acted more quickly to address the situation publicly. They needed to demonstrate their commitment to cleanliness and food safety, and reassure customers that this was an isolated event, and that no tampered-with food was actually delivered to customers.

On the other hand, if we look at the Wells Fargo crisis discussed in previous chapters, we see that no matter how well-crafted the bank's crisis communications were—all their proactive communication initiatives, their promises and words of compassion—nothing mattered until the bank finally took the right actions behind the scenes to manage their cultural crisis.

The bank's thoughtfully crafted crisis communications didn't fool anyone, least of all Congress. Why? Because it was evident that the problem ran deep, and that the communications were a shallow Band-Aid. I would even go as far as calling them an attempted decoy. A decoy to save the then-CEO John Stumpf's reputation and position at the company. The bank apologized and attempted to fix a deeply rooted cultural crisis by adding safeguards, such as email confirmations when new customer accounts are made—safeguards that should have already been in place, might I add—and it simply wasn't enough to fix the much deeper, fundamental problem. Nobody bought it until the bank admitted to a cultural crisis and Stumpf left his position.

Let's look at both these examples through the CRP lens:

Domino's Pizza waited two days to communicate effectively, which led to an otherwise preventable escalation. The restaurant in question closed, and national sales dropped. If we plug the numbers into the CRP equation for nationwide material impact, we're looking at a year-long impact of 1%-2% divided by a two-day communication delay, which equals 0.5%-1% of nationwide sales impact per day of delayed response. In other words, this two-day mistake ended up impacting a *year* of sales. What would you think if your organization lost 1% of its yearly sales for *each day* of an easily avoidable, poor decision?

The Wells Fargo case is a little harder to calculate, as there are many factors. For example, this was a deep-seated cultural crisis that led to the organization committing fraud. It's not the same scale of crisis as the Domino's Pizza incident. However, if we want to evaluate monetary impact due to this crisis (and its wrongdoing), John Stumpf had to forgo $41 million[26] of previously promised compensation, and Wells Fargo received a $185 million fine. Additionally, the bank's chief financial officer, John Shrewsberry, reported in March 2017 that the bank had been spending between $40 and $50 million[27] on subject matter expert consultants, including lawyers, each quarter since the scandal broke. The reality is that these repercussions were inevitable, due to the nature of the crisis. They are not dependent on the bank's response to the crisis. Instead, they are dependent on the fact that the bank should have prevented this fraudulent activity from happening in the first place. In other words, having a crisis ready culture would have mitigated this material impact.

However, the bank could have mitigated the soft CRP impact to some extent had it taken the right approach in its initial response to the incident, as mentioned above. A study conducted by the management consultancy firm, cg42, a few months after the scandal had broken, revealed that the reputational impact on the bank was significant. The study revealed that negative perception of the bank had increased to 52% post-scandal, compared to 15% pre-scandal; and of the non-customers surveyed, 54% said they were unlikely to consider becoming customers of the bank in the future, compared to 22% prior to the crisis occurring.[28]

What I love about the contrast of these two examples is that they eloquently demonstrate the two critical components to successful crisis management:

1. The actions you take behind the scenes to manage the actual incident that occurred; and

2. The way you choose to communicate those actions and other details regarding the crisis and its management with your key stakeholders.

Your crisis management success depends on your ability to effectively do both these things well and simultaneously. Failing on either account results in the failure of your overall crisis management. In order to be in a position to successfully manage both ends, you need to take the deep dive approach that I am about to share with you.

So, without further ado, let's dive in, shall we?

THE DEEP-DIVE PROCESS

One of the great things about this deep-dive process is that, each time I undergo the exercise with my clients, not only do we equip ourselves with a comprehensive understanding of their most pertinent and relevant risks, but we uncover many different elements that serve to benefit the organization far beyond solely crisis management. This is, in part, why I'm so passionate about crisis preparedness, and particularly of taking this "deep-dive" approach. By approaching crisis preparedness in this very thorough way, you will naturally:

- Learn more about your stakeholders and how to strengthen the relationships you share with them. This benefits everything from your marketing and PR initiatives to sales, customer service, reputation management, and more.

- Identify hidden gaps which, once filled, end up benefitting and strengthening the organization's daily activities and capabilities. For example, organizations often lack an efficient, streamlined way of communicating with their entire internal population at once. In a crisis, having this capability is very important. Even outside a crisis, this capability can be incredibly beneficial. Guess what? Developing or improving this capability is part of the deep-dive process! Another example that comes to mind is work that I did with a client in the financial industry. Through the deep-dive process, we realized there were gaps in the organization's investor agreements and side letters that left the company exposed in the event of one of their high-risk scenarios. You can imagine how quickly the organization took measures to mitigate that exposure!

- Boost company morale and help create strong bonds between departments. The deep-dive process is a very interactive exercise. You need engagement from each department, which can be atypical for many organizations in their daily activities. It is therefore often a great cross-organization team-building initiative. After all, the company that prepares together wins together!

While you read the next chapters and undertake the exercises I lay out, I am confident you will experience some "aha!" moments of your own and discover ways to benefit your organization far beyond the sole topic or task of crisis management. And, please, when that happens, I'd love to hear about it!

That having been said, let's start diving into your first high-risk scenario. I recommend tackling one high-risk scenario at a time. This means that, while there will be some overlap, for the most part you should undertake the exercises found in this and the next chapter for each of your high-risk scenarios. This is the best way to build out a robust and comprehensive program.

DEVELOPING YOUR CRISIS READY PLAYBOOKS

The first of the two components required for successful crisis management is the behind-the-scenes portion of your crisis preparedness. I refer to this portion as your crisis ready playbooks. Playbooks contain all the action plans and resources that will help guide your crisis management team through the first twenty-four to forty-eight hours of a breaking crisis.

Unlike the foundation of your program, which we developed in chapter five, your crisis ready playbooks are in-the-moment crisis management resources for your team. This means they need to incorporate anything of possible advantage to your team in the heat of the moment. In order for the playbooks to be effective, they also need to be short and concise. A common challenge is including the important elements while also keeping the playbooks trim and fit; you don't want your crisis management team to be poring over hundreds of pages of documentation. Focusing only on necessary elements should be your priority. Anything left after trimming the fat belongs in either the foundation of your program or nowhere at all!

Because there are many pieces required to develop your crisis ready playbooks, the best way for me to make this real and interesting for you (I hope!) is to help you get started in actually developing your first playbook. Instead of simply talking about what you should do, we are going to go through the process together so that, by the end of this chapter, you have a preliminary draft of your playbook that you can continue to strengthen.

To do this, let's choose a common high-risk scenario that applies to every organization nowadays: a cybersecurity incident.

While there are many aspects to a cybersecurity crisis that we will not cover in this book, such as your IT department's incident response planning or the legal aspects of managing a cybersecurity crisis, what we *are* going to do is focus on getting you to start thinking through all the key decisions, factors, and actions that will need to be considered and implemented by the members of your crisis management team.

You'll soon learn that cybersecurity crises are not simple black-and-white events. In fact, they can have many grey zones and variables. For this reason, the last thing you want is to tackle the preparedness process of this scenario (or any of your high-risk scenarios) in a vacuum. The closer you work and collaborate with the appropriate members of your legal, compliance, IT, operations, communications, HR, and other departments, the more robust and practical your preparedness will be. By this point in this book, you probably foresaw me saying this!

COLLECTING THE NECESSARY INFORMATION

In order to create your crisis ready playbooks, you need to make sure you have all the necessary information regarding the scenario. Your objective is to have a holistic understanding of what a cybersecurity crisis is, and what challenges your team will face. This means you need to conduct interviews and have discussions with the right people.

Since I develop the foundation of the program and the first scenario's playbook and handbook simultaneously, I have the advantage of being able to merge all the necessary discussions into one meeting with each team member rather than having several conversations with the same people, saving everyone from unnecessary redundancy. Laying the groundwork and accumulating bigger pieces of the puzzle in this fashion saves time and effort.

It's time to prepare for those meetings. Some questions will be common to each meeting, while others will be department- or function-specific. Use the questions below as a starting point. There is no such thing as a stupid question. If you can think it and you don't know the answer, then don't be too shy to ask the right person.

As for who to speak with, I'll leave it to you to decide who the best people are to have these discussions with—though don't forget about that list you made in chapter five!

Baseline questions to answer:

- At what point would a cybersecurity incident become a corporate crisis?

- What are the data and systems that, if breached, would immediately represent a corporate crisis for your organization (a.k.a. the organization's "crown jewels")?

- What are some escalation factors that can affect the management of a cybersecurity crisis?

- What are some of the complications that can occur that would make the team's crisis management tasks more difficult?

- Are there subcategories for this scenario that may affect your strategy for response? (More on this in chapter seven.)

- What are the roles, responsibilities, and action items each department, division and / or region will be responsible for, during the first twenty-four to forty-eight hours of this type of crisis? Does each department currently have everything they need to complete each task efficiently?

- How does a cybersecurity crisis risk affecting the organization's different stakeholder groups?

- What are the key concerns that you can anticipate each stakeholder group having, in the event of this scenario? (In other words, what will matter to them?)

- What are the legal and / or regulatory risks or impacts that the organization needs to be aware of?

- What are the reputational risks associated with this scenario?

- What can the organization do now, or prepare to do, in order to mitigate these risks or potential impacts?

- Are there third-party experts that should be consulted now that would help the team manage this type of crisis? Examples may include the organization's outside PR agency, outside legal counsel, forensic experts, crisis management experts, law enforcement, etc.

- What types of resources may the team require or benefit from that should be included within the playbook?

Make sure to work closely with your IT department and design your cybersecurity crisis management playbook to align with their cybersecurity incident management procedures. It's important that both components use the same language and that the levels of crisis management are in sync. The last thing you want while managing a crisis is for not everyone to be on the same page. This means ensuring alignment on everything from levels of severity, language, and terminology, to crisis management approaches.

DEFINING YOUR INTERNAL ESCALATION PROCESS

Depending on your organization's type and size, your IT department may deal with a number of cybersecurity incidents on a regular basis. Few of them, if any, get to crisis level. But what if one does? What should your IT department do?

This goes back to determining who belongs within this scenario's assessment group. The question then becomes, who should your IT team call upon to help them assess the potential scope and impact of the incident? What should the team do from there, if they deem it worthy of escalation? Should it be directly escalated to leadership? Or should there be another layer of assessment before it reaches that point?

Once that group and their process has been defined, arm them with important criteria, factors, and questions they can use to help them assess the situation and rightfully determine if it needs to be escalated. For example, are there specific types of data or systems that, if breached, require an immediate escalation? What other potential impacts should they be considering, assessing, and evaluating? This can include things like specific types of impacts on people, systems, operations, or legal liability.

By having conversations with different members of the crisis team, you should be able to gather the information needed to create a series of questions to help the assessment group assess the scope and potential impact of the situation. Following is an example of what to include within this questionnaire:

Assessing the potential impact of a cybersecurity incident

If you can answer "yes" to any of the following questions, promptly escalate the situation to the appropriate members of the crisis management team.

- Does the situation directly affect the organization's ability to conduct business? For example, does it render key systems inoperable, or threaten to?

- Does the situation risk negatively affecting the organization's stakeholders? For example, has personally identifiable information (PII) or personal health information (PHI) been breached?

- Does the situation risk negatively affecting the organization's reputation over the long term? For example, does it risk resulting in a loss of key stakeholder trust in the organization?

- Does the situation risk presenting legal and / or regulatory repercussions to the organization? For example, could it result in a potential lawsuit or regulatory investigation?

If the assessment group determines that the incident is at crisis level—in accordance with your organization's definition of a corporate crisis (ahem, remember what you learned in chapter four?)—the next step is to lay out a simple escalation process for them to follow. In other words, determine who they need to escalate the incident to next. Some organizations want the "responsible group" to be the next filtering level, while others want to escalate immediately to the leadership group. Work with your team to decide on the next course of action that makes sense for your organization.

The goal is to ensure that the right eyes and minds are in the room. This process needs to enable quick and intuitive escalation when the situation merits it, while also avoiding unnecessary escalation.

What if IT isn't the first to detect that something fishy is going on, and the organization's systems or data may be in jeopardy? Do the rest of your departments know that they should immediately report any suspicious technological activity to the IT department—and do they know how to go about reporting it? Something to consider...and train the rest of the team on.

PIECING IT TOGETHER

Once you have had the necessary conversations, collected the data, and developed the processes that need to take place in order to declare a crisis, it is time to develop your cybersecurity crisis ready playbook. Let's walk through this process together, section by section.

As there will be one playbook for each of your high-risk scenarios, you should give them the same structure, style, and flow. The structure, style, and flow that I've developed over time is what you'll find throughout the coming pages. Feel free to adapt it to better fit your organization.

SECTION 1: PLAN ACTIVATION

This is a short section meant to provide your team with the information needed to declare a crisis and activate your crisis management team and program. Depending on the scenario and your organization's preferences, some, or all, of the following should be included:

Playbook activation guidelines

This includes a high-level overview of the scenario and the criteria that defines the high-risk scenario as a crisis for the organization. If in doubt, refer to chapter four where we discuss these defining criteria.

You may also want to include clearly defined levels of crisis management, so your team can quickly categorize the incident's level of severity. Your levels might look something like this:

BUSINESS AS USUAL LEVEL	• Incident does not present, or is unlikely to present, a crisis to the organization. • Team performs their responsibilities as usual.
STANDBY LEVEL	• Incident has a heightened likelihood of presenting a crisis to the organization. • Assessment group to convene and examine potential scope of the situation, escalating or monitoring the situation as appropriate.
ACTIVATION LEVEL	• Incident presents a crisis to the organization. • Crisis management team and program are activated by appropriate parties.

If you decide to include this type of categorization, make sure the levels are consistent across all types of crises. Build this element into your program as a whole, and then tweak it based on the scenario.

Phone tree and conference line numbers

When a crisis is declared, how does the crisis management team become notified? When do they gather to discuss the incident and agree on next steps? If the crisis strikes during work hours this will be relatively simple, but if it strikes during an evening, weekend, or holiday, then what? Include protocols for notifying and gathering team members in this section.

Internal escalation process

This is where you include the process for identifying, evaluating, and escalating a detected incident. It is important not to use cumbersome language. Instead, try to lay out the process in a visual diagram, flowchart, or table that quickly defines and demonstrates this process at a glance.

Governance overview

This should be a quick visual representation of your crisis management teams and their members, for easy reference. (This can also be placed in the appendix of your playbook.)

Timeline or roadmap of the first 24 hours of a breaking crisis

At a glance, what are the big action items that need to happen during the first twenty-four hours of crisis management? Is it possible to create a visual timeline or roadmap that the team can reference to get an overall, general, and approximate idea of the key events that need to unfold?

Note: This is not something you can put together until after developing your action plans and crisis communication strategy.

SECTION 2: ACTION PLANS

Each member of your team will turn to this section when a crisis is declared. The action plans house all the behind-the-scenes tasks that successful crisis management requires. The way you organize this section will depend on your governance structure. For example, you may have one dedicated action plan for each department.

It is important to provide each group, team, or department with a dedicated action list—or task consideration list—that they can leverage to help guide their decisions. These action plans or task considerations should include:

- Prioritized key action items that each team member is responsible for implementing or overseeing, in the first twenty-four to forty-eight hours of the crisis.

- Designation of a clear "owner" for each task.

- If possible, an approximate timeline for implementation. For example, under a column titled "ideal timeline," I may consider including something along the lines of, "goal: within one hour from the time the crisis occurs," or "ongoing," or "as quickly as possible." This timeline may end up changing in the heat of the moment, but it's good for team members to have an idea of what an ideal timeline looks like.

I always include a line that says something about the timeline being indicative and that it will need to be adapted depending on the specifics of the incident. Including this note will likely make your legal team happy!

Sometimes an organization's legal department is less inclined to develop crisis management action plans for certain high-risk scenarios. This is because they are concerned with liability. For example, they may be worried about a situation in which the organization did not permit every step of the action plans to be performed. From their legally trained perspective, the lawyers' concern is that the company might be held accountable for not doing what is specified within the action plans. They don't want to put the organization in a position where someone can say, "your crisis plan said to do this, and you didn't do it."

To help the legal department feel more comfortable, I work around this risk by playing with terminology. I find that calling an action plan something more suggestive, such as a "task consideration list," is helpful. I generally include a footnote that says something like, "the following task considerations are not all-inclusive and need to be adapted to the specifics of the situation," which helps me ensure the crisis team has what they need in the heat of the moment while also helping the legal department feel comfortable with a more suggestive approach to crisis planning.

Action plans can't be developed without the help and input of the collective. This is another area where interviews, discussions, and team building comes in. Each high-risk scenario will require different actions, since there is no one-size-fits-all crisis management strategy. This is another reason why the deep-dive approach is so valuable: it enables you to understand the scenario and its potential variables, and to have the difficult discussions when you have the luxury of time and contemplation.

Some of these discussions can be difficult, as there are crisis scenarios that are less cut and dry, and even more controversial. Using cybersecurity as an example, there are many variables that can come into play. Variables that you probably won't even be aware of until you have the required discussions with the different members of your team, such as:

- What would the team do if it was aware of a cybersecurity breach, but knew that it would take months before the organization would have any real answers to both the business's and stakeholders' questions? What should the course of action be? What would the legal or regulatory obligations be, and how would the organization comply with them?

- What if the team had answers, but the FBI didn't allow the organization to take any actions or communicate with impacted parties? While the team would have no choice but to comply, what if stakeholders risked seeing this compliance as a disservice to them, and the organization risked losing their trust and relationships as a result?

Other high-risk scenarios present even more difficulty because of emotion. For example, what if your organization found itself in a situation where a high-profile member of leadership was arrested or accused of a crime that had nothing to do with the organization, but presented a controversy in regards to the values and ethics of the brand itself? How would you manage this type of crisis? Would you immediately distance the organization from the executive? What if you believed they were innocent, and wrongfully accused? At what point would you draw a line, and at what point might that line change from either perspective?

What about a situation like Uber? I've been saying for years that the co-founder and former CEO of the car transportation company, Travis Kalanick, *was* the organization's crisis. He was what was wrong, on so many levels. Yet it took years and multiple viral issues, scandals, and even crises for the board to finally come to this conclusion, and for Kalanick to finally resign from his position.

> **All those years of viral and controversial issues, layered one on top of the other, left an a cumulative soft CRP impact on the Uber brand and its reputation. This soft CRP resulted in things like lost customers, continued negative news coverage, empowered competitors, multiple fines in different countries, and more.**

At the time of this writing, the situation is too fresh to know what steps Uber will take to repair their image and move forward on a positive, crisis-free path. However, it is easy to see and understand that removing Kalanick from his position was a difficult decision. It is easy to be too close to a situation and for an answer that may be clear to outside professionals to not be clear to those responsible for making the decision. It can also be a very challenging decision to make. What would your organization do in a similarly challenging situation?

Bringing these types of potential scenarios to the table now will save a lot of time and heartache down the road. On the other hand, there will also be some simpler questions to answer, as part of your crisis management tasks. Returning to the example scenario of a cybersecurity crisis, these simpler tasks to identify include things like:

- In the event of a cybersecurity crisis, at what point will you call in a forensics team? Do you have a team vetted and ready to hire? Who will be responsible for making this call and owning this relationship?

- What about the FBI and / or your insurance provider? At what point are you required to notify each of these parties? Who will be responsible for making these calls and owning these relationships?

- What do the law and / or regulatory agencies require you to do? Does it depend on jurisdictions? Do you know what and when those jurisdictions come into play and, if not, have you armed the organization with a third-party expert who can help you with this?

- What will each department's crisis management role look like? Is it dependent on what is breached and its potential impact? What might this look like?

A big part of being crisis ready is understanding the full breadth and scope of your high-risk scenarios, exploring all realistic and likely variables, having the difficult discussions now, and drawing up practical action plans and resources that will help successfully guide the team as it manages the crisis. Now is the time to do this.

As a consultant, I approach the development of these action plans and task considerations by first talking with each member of the predefined crisis management team, and then using that information to develop their respective crisis management action plans. Once the action plans have been created, I sit back down with each team member, one by one, to discuss their respective action plan and to gain their feedback. Once their feedback is implemented, I go through another round of reviews with the leadership team to gain full approval.

SECTION 3: COMMUNICATION STRATEGY

A scenario-specific crisis communication strategy, and its pre-drafted messaging, belongs in your crisis communication handbook. This is typically a separate document from your playbook, owned by your crisis communications team, but I like to at least reference each scenario's communications strategy within the playbook to benefit the rest of the team. Here's why.

Every member of the crisis management team will have access to the playbooks. However, only a subset group (the communications department, for example) will have access to the crisis communication handbook. The reason for this is that they will be the ones responsible for drafting and finalizing the organization's crisis communications. Therefore, by including a high-level view of the organization's crisis communication approach, you are providing everybody else with an "at a glance" understanding of what they can expect.

This high-level overview may include things like:

- A list of key stakeholders, and which team members are responsible for communicating with them.

- A decision tree detailing when the organization should be reactive versus proactive in their crisis communication outreach, and with whom.

- A selection of different means of crisis communication, organized by stakeholder group.

In the next chapter, we are going to develop your crisis communication handbook together. Once the handbooks are developed, you can decide which aspects you would like to include in your playbooks.

SECTION 4: CONTACT INFORMATION

This one might seem straightforward, but we aren't talking about a simple phonebook here. When putting together your contact information, include *all* relevant information for quick and easy access in the heat of the moment. Who to include varies from organization to organization, but some suggestions include:

- All members of the crisis management team and their alternates.

- Third party experts and key vendors you may need to contact during the management of the crisis.

- Tier one stakeholders, especially if there is a specific subset group that a high-level executive will need to call, who may not work with the organization's CRM or other database in their day-to-day activities.

Some of you might already have a CRM or other databases or systems that house the necessary contact information for one or more of your stakeholder groups. If this is the case, tag the appropriate data for easy reference, access, and filtering. Be sure to reference the systems, by providing a link or other point of entry in this section of your playbooks. Finally, keep a hardcopy backup. If your systems go down during a crisis, you don't want to be undone by a loose cable!

SECTION 5: RESOURCE REPOSITORY

Here is where you get to be creative! This section is for helpful information and resources that will facilitate the team's crisis management when things are going crazy. What does your team need? It might not be possible to foresee every circumstance, situation, or need, but the goal is to do your best to include anything helpful that you can think of. The more interviews you conduct for each scenario, the better you'll be able to answer this question.

Some resource suggestions include:

Important lists

For example, in the event of a cybersecurity incident, what constitutes the organization's critical data and systems, that, if breached, would constitute a crisis for the organization?

Timelines, flowcharts, and other visual references

For example, if your organization has investors, is there a point in time when a special redemption timeline would come into play? What does that timeline look like? What circumstances might trigger it? Is it possible to create a flowchart or visual timeline that provides your team with a simple understanding of these conditions and how they might play out?

Specific stakeholder agreements or side letters

Are there specific agreements or side letters that you particularly want to call your team's attention to? If so, include a high-level overview of them within this section of your playbook.

Links and references

This may include important links to outside websites or resources that team members can reference. However, I suggest refraining from keeping actual access credentials within these documents for their protection and security.

I was not kidding when I said that there is a lot of work to be done for each high-risk scenario. I hope you can see the value in undertaking this deep-dive. Whether you're reading through for the first time, or actually implementing what you learn (here's hoping for the latter, whether now or in the near future), you've made it through six intense chapters. I think you deserve a break, don't you? With that in mind, let's pause, and interrupt our program for a moment to bring you this story...

INTERLUDE

I was a strange kid. (I would argue I was an adorable kid, but a strange one nonetheless.) The thing that was strange about me was— or rather, is—the way my mind worked. I was the kid who saw risk *everywhere*. Not in a hide-under-the-bed-and-never-come-out sort of way, but in a weary, "is the juice really worth the squeeze?" kind of way.

It was beyond my control. My mind would automatically spot risks, sometimes in the strangest of moments. For example, I would make my parents taste my food before I ate it, in case it had been poisoned.

Apparently, I figured better them than me. Sorry, Mom and Dad! (In my defense, I was about six years old...and yes, I *did* evaluate the risk of you deciding I am a terrible human being by telling you this!) It was not a conscious effort. It was natural and unavoidable. And while I was a good older sister, protective and loving with my younger sister Stephanie, thinking back now I realize that I must have been a total and utter drag to her. (Sorry, Stephy!)

We didn't have much money growing up. So, an evening that involved dinner and a movie out on the town was a rare treat. Most normal children in my position would see it as a lucky treat. Maybe even an exciting one. But remember, I was strange. I must have been about eight years old, and my dad asked my sister and me if we wanted to go out for dinner and then to see a movie. In the moment that it took my sister to shout "Yeah!" and start bouncing around with excitement, my mind had already spotted the risk.

If we went out for dinner and a movie, that meant we had to go downtown. But my dad didn't have a car at the time, which meant we needed to take the subway (or the "metro," as we call it in Montreal). The metro is a dangerous place. My sister could fall into the tracks, or get lost, or worse, be kidnapped. Everything was made worse by the fact that, even if we made it into the city unscathed, we had to come back home in the middle of the night. This meant we needed to get back on the metro *in the middle of the night!* For my eight-year-old self, this risk definitely did not outweigh the benefit.

"Nope, I'm good. Let's just stay in tonight," was my reply. I mean, clearly you can understand why!

It was no wonder when my dad came up with a song for me. To this day, I can vividly picture him opening his eyes wide, crouching down towards my level and singing: "Paranoia will destroy ya. Paranoia will destroy ya!" to me in a funny, sort of robotic voice. Can you hear the tune in your head? It's very catchy, isn't it?

The truth is that I'm still that strange kid. I still see risk everywhere. It really is how my mind works. The good news is that I managed to turn this unique trait (apparently not everyone can relate to this?) into a career. And I think it is part of the reason why I'm so passionate about what I do. I help organizations spot and understand risk, and then I get to help them prevent and prepare for it. This way, they *can* go out for dinner and to see that movie, knowing that they've done everything in their power to mitigate, control, and prepare for the downsides.

The other benefit is that I now have an excuse. When sudden and irrational things come out of my mouth and the people I'm with start looking at me strangely, hoping to slowly back up and walk away because they think I am crazy, I can just plead: "Crisis management!" And the crazy glares turn into laughter!

Alright, so there you have it. A little strange tidbit about me. Go ahead, feel free to laugh. Feel free to even walk up to me singing the paranoia song, because it's guaranteed you'll make *me* laugh! But that's enough about me... let's get back to you and your crisis readiness, because after all, that's the whole reason we're here.

As we saw at the start of chapter six, getting the behind-the-scenes management right will only take you halfway to crisis management success. The other half depends on your ability to communicate effectively with those who matter most to your organization. Your organization should strive to be *the* authority on its own crises, and we still have work to do to achieve this. That is what the latter half of this book is all about.

So, without further ado, let's return to our regular program.

07

WHEN TO TALK AND WHEN TO SHUT UP

Do you remember the crisis Samsung faced in 2016? The one where their Galaxy Note7 smartphones were bursting into flames, putting customers in harm's way? This crisis escalated to the point where the U.S. Federal Aviation Administration (FAA) advised passengers not to turn on or charge their

Note7 phones onboard an aircraft, nor to stow them in the plane's cargo. Talk about an inconvenience for customers and an unwanted event that risked destroying Samsung's good name in the mobile device industry!

A month after the big unveiling of the highly-anticipated Galaxy Note7 phones, Samsung announced the recall of over 2.5 million devices globally, wiping out over $14.3 billion[29] of the South Korean company's market capitalization. This was a worst nightmare come true.

In October 2016, less than two months after its launch, Samsung announced that it would stop producing the Galaxy Note7 phone altogether. They also said that the company expected to experience a hit of around $3 billion to their operating profits for the last quarter of 2016 and the first of 2017 combined because of the phone's discontinuation. Reuters called the situation, "one of the costliest product safety failures in tech history."

This was a major crisis for Samsung. Yet, right from the start, Samsung proved they had their priorities straight. Their timely, informative communications demonstrated that they cared more about their customers' safety than anything else. Samsung knew how important their communications were going to be to help them manage this crisis and get ahead of the story.

However, even with the best intentions, their laudable communications ended up being one of their crisis management downfalls. For example, Samsung was quick to tell their Hong Kong customers that their phones would not be affected. Unfortunately, they spoke too soon. The next day the company had to retract that statement, alerting customers that 500 phones in Hong Kong were impacted after all. This misinformation and retraction confused their customers.

Meanwhile, in the United States, Samsung issued a recall of their affected phones. They were so proactive in issuing this recall that they neglected to comply with regulatory requirements, which state that these types of recalls must be called in collaboration with the appropriate regulatory agencies. Samsung jumped the gun, which led to the brand frustrating regulators, who happened to be very public with their frustrations. For example, the U.S. Consumer Product Safety Commission chairperson, Elliot F. Kaye, said at a news conference:

> I will say as a general matter that it's not a recipe for a successful recall for a company to go out on its own," and he continued to insinuate that organizations that believe they can conduct successful recalls without the necessary coordination with the appropriate government entities "need to have more than their phone checked."

Each time Samsung made a communication mistake that resulted in a retraction, a confusion, or a frustration, the media of course ate it up. The media was eager to bring the crisis back to the forefront of the news cycle and publicly criticize the organization for their lack of effective crisis management.

What you say, how you say it, and when you say it are all critical components of crisis communication. They directly affect the ultimate success of your crisis management. As we have learned from Samsung, this is not always an easy task. Even with the best intentions, you can end up making mistakes that negatively affect your reputation, which leads to affecting your bottom line.

The challenge does not end there. As you may very well be able to imagine—or rather, foresee—there is often an internal struggle when it comes to successfully balancing stakeholders' crisis communication demands, such as transparency and timeliness, with gathering the necessary facts so that your communications are accurate. While stakeholders' demands are real and important, as we explored in chapter three, the truth is that you won't have all the facts confirmed at the onset of

CRISIS READY RULE

One poor statement (or tweet) can undermine an entire crisis management strategy.

a crisis. You just simply won't. So, how can you strive to successfully achieve the right balance?

The good news is that with all the work you've done throughout the previous six chapters—from the discussions you've had, to understanding who your stakeholders are and what they will expect of your organization in times of crisis, straight through to understanding the challenges and realities that await your team in a crisis—you have most of what you'll need to develop an effective and balanced crisis communication strategy.

BEING STRATEGIC

Never communicate just for the sake of communicating. You need to be strategic when it comes to crisis communication, which means you need to have a defined purpose. While your goals and objectives will vary slightly depending on the situation and scenario, for the most part the whole point of communicating effectively is to:

- Get ahead of the story and own, to the greatest extent possible, the narrative of your own crisis.

- Ensure consistency in messaging across all departments, regions, and stakeholders.

- Provide key stakeholders with timely, transparent, and compassionate communications that reinforce the organization's commitment to them and its values.

- Position your organization as the voice of trust, credibility, and leadership throughout the management of the crisis.

To achieve these goals, you need to begin by having an established and practical internal process for drafting, finalizing, and disseminating your crisis communications to the right people throughout the organization. You also need to have an established alignment with the right members of the crisis management team, so that everyone understands the important role the organization's crisis communications will play in the event of a crisis. It is necessary that all pertinent members agree on and approve of each communication strategy.

In my experience, it can be a challenge to get certain people and departments on board with taking a timely and informative approach to communicating in a crisis. While this challenge can present itself for several reasons, the two most common reasons are:

Legal hesitations

Legal professionals, whether internal or outside counsel, are tasked with protecting the organization from legal exposure and risk. As a result, taking a proactive crisis communication approach can sometimes be counterintuitive to them, which can sometimes lead to resistance. For this reason, it is important that you have the necessary discussions with these members of your team long before a crisis strikes. You want to understand their perspective, objectives, and challenges, just as you want them to properly understand yours. Alignment and approval should come before, not during or after, a crisis.

Ignorance

Sometimes, when an organization has been around for a while, they may have encountered some issues or crises along the way. Leadership may have chosen to communicate in a very minimalistic way, or maybe not at all. They may have even chosen to bury their heads in the sand, hoping for the issue to go away on its own. And perhaps it went away, but times have changed. The realities and challenges discussed in chapter two are sometimes foreign, or even unknown, to executives who are of the opinion that if something worked in the past, it will work in the future. This simply isn't the case. Being aware of this doesn't always make our task of gaining the necessary approvals any easier, however.

If you can relate to these two common internal challenges, you may want to jump back towards the end of chapter two, where I provided you with some strategic tips on overcoming these types of internal obstacles and gaining the required buy-in from leadership and other members of your team. Trust me; if there is even a hint that it will be difficult for you to gain the communications buy-in that the situation calls for, it's worth dealing with that risk now rather than having it block you in the future.

I also want you to know that if you find yourself in this type of position, you are far from being alone. There are always ways to approach and overcome these internal challenges in a progressive manner. So, don't be discouraged. Instead, be strategic!

BUILDING YOUR COMMUNICATIONS TEAM

Within your crisis management governance structure, you should have assigned a team responsible for your organization's crisis communications. Depending on the size and type of your organization, this team may consist of anywhere from a couple people to a dozen or more. If the latter applies to you, you are going to want to assign specific crisis communication roles and responsibilities to each member. If your team is on the small side, then one or more members of your crisis communications team will simply be required to wear more than one hat.

Both scenarios can work well, so long as everybody has a full understanding of their roles and responsibilities, and how they fit into the bigger picture. These roles and responsibilities will include things like:

- Drafting the organization's crisis communications.

- Having the drafted crisis communications approved by the correct people, in a timely fashion.

- Disseminating your organization's crisis communications to all relevant stakeholder owners.

- Monitoring and engaging on social media and other communication platforms.

- Receiving and responding to media inquiries.

- Translating approved messages into different languages, as needed.

As we saw with the Fort McMurray wildfires in chapter five, two people were responsible for drafting and disseminating the communications that helped 88,000 people evacuate their homes in just a few hours. This is a good example of how, no matter the size of your crisis communications team, if you have the right people who clearly understand their roles and responsibilities, combined with the right communication strategy, you can always deliver. Designating the right people, developing the right strategy, and effectively training the team to be crisis ready is paramount—the latter being something we'll explore in more detail in chapter nine.

Start thinking about who within your crisis communications team you're going to assign to each of the above-mentioned roles and responsibilities, along with any other roles that may apply to your organization's crisis communication needs. Consistent with your organization's governance structure, assign an alternate team member to each primary member of the team, in the event that the main person is not available to take on his or her role in the heat of the moment.

How will

the crisis communications team quickly disseminate the approved crisis communications to each relevant stakeholder owner, and effectively meet your stated crisis communication goals?

DEVELOPING PRACTICAL INTERNAL PROCESSES

After assigning roles and responsibilities, the next step is to develop strong internal processes that will help your team effectively perform their tasks. The goal here, as always, is to develop practical processes that will enable your team to efficiently meet your crisis communication goals and objectives. This means your team needs to be able to quickly and effectively:

- Finalize the organization's crisis communications.

- Have the communications approved by the right people.

- Modify the communications based on the feedback from the approval team.

- Disseminate the approved communications to all relevant stakeholder owners, so that they may begin to communicate with the stakeholders whose relationships they own.

In my experience, drafting and gaining approval are simpler processes, partly because many organizations already have a system in place, though you may need to streamline the current processes for efficiency. Additionally, we will draft a good portion of your key message points as a part of developing your scenario-specific crisis communication handbooks. Therefore, your team shouldn't be starting from scratch at the onset of a crisis.

The part that can be more challenging is developing the internal dissemination process. However, the complexity of this task depends on the size and structure of your organization. Ultimately, the question you want to answer is: How will the crisis communications team quickly disseminate the approved crisis communications to each relevant stakeholder owner, and effectively meet your stated crisis communication goals?

If you already have a process that you can leverage for this, test it out!

Strengthen any gaps or kinks you may identify. If, like many organizations, you don't have an efficient preexisting process to leverage, you have some work to do.

You did some homework in chapter three, so you already have a list of your key stakeholders and their owners. You've also had conversations with your stakeholder owners, where you discussed the ways they communicate with their teams and amongst one another. Use this information to figure out the most practical way to provide the approved communications to all stakeholder owners. Ideally, this should happen all at once. You want one streamlined process here, not numerous disparate ones.

This process should arm the crisis communications team with a quick and direct way to provide each stakeholder owner with the approved crisis communications, so they can quickly and efficiently commence communication with their key stakeholders. And remember: communication just isn't communication if only one side is talking; enable two-way communication capabilities. Part of your stakeholder owners' crisis management tasks will be to monitor, triage, and notify the crisis communications team of incoming inquiries and comments, as well as any speculation or rumors that may be rising or circulating. As part of this process, you want to make sure they have an intuitive way to do this. Finally, be sure to develop a backup process in case systems go down. In the event of a cybersecurity incident, natural disaster, or terrorist attack, will you still be able to finalize, approve, and disseminate the organization's crisis communications? The answer needs to be yes!

Concept to reality

I have a client that is a big name in the manufacturing industry. They are a global brand with over 10,000 employees worldwide. When we began working together, I quickly learned two important things. The first was that they did not have a consolidated list of all their key stakeholder groups. (This is extremely common. I have actually never encountered a client who did.) The second was that they did not have an efficient way to communicate with all stakeholder owners—nor the entire company population, but more on this one later—at once. When needed, they would use many different forms of communication and hope to reach everyone. In times of crisis, we don't want to *hope*. We want to be efficient, effective, and confident in our processes. We want surety to the greatest extent possible.

Thus, before we could begin diving into developing strategies, we had to establish the organization's crisis communications goal and develop an efficient and practical process for disseminating their crisis communications to all those who would need them. The two dozen interviews I conducted at the onset of this project helped me understand who the organization's key stakeholder groups were, how their owners communicate—or oversee communication—during daily business hours, what procedural gaps were present, and how we could leverage existing strengths.

This data provided me with what I needed to develop a practical and efficient internal crisis communication dissemination process. Here's what that process looks like, for this particular organization:

- In the event of a crisis, a designated person within the organization's crisis communications team is responsible for drafting the organization's crisis communications, having them approved by the right people, and disseminating the approved messaging to all stakeholder owners. We're going to call this person Sheila.

- By identifying all the organization's key stakeholders, we also identified all key stakeholder owners. We then determined that a stakeholder owner distribution list would be the most effective and ideal way to get the approved messaging to this list of roughly two dozen people company-wide. So, we created this distribution list and assigned someone with the responsibility of keeping it current.

- We also pre-drafted a distribution email for Sheila to leverage in times of crisis, as part of the organization's crisis communication handbooks. This email draft includes important directives and reminders that we want stakeholder owners to have top of mind at the onset of a crisis. Of course, in the event of a crisis part of Sheila's responsibility is to revise and finalize this email draft, but she has a solid template to work from, helping her streamline her dissemination task.

- From there, we trained all stakeholder owners to be familiar with the crisis communication process—to know exactly what they can expect, as well as what will be expected of them, in times of crisis.

- We also set up an alternative distribution list on a separate server that Sheila can use in the event that the organization's systems are down during a crisis.

Developing your internal crisis communication dissemination process is critical for your crisis management success. This becomes relatively simple when you take the time to understand and collect the required information. Before you know it, you will have determined the most practical and efficient ways to develop and implement this element of your crisis preparedness.

DEVELOPING PRACTICAL EXTERNAL PROCESSES

Once you have your internal dissemination process established, the next step is to develop the best strategy for effectively communicating with each of your stakeholder groups during a real-time crisis. Let's begin by discussing *how* you will communicate with each of your stakeholders in a crisis. Remember, you want to anticipate their needs and meet them on their turf.

In order to do this, look at each one of your stakeholder groups and the data you collected on them as part of your chapter three homework and answer the following questions, one stakeholder group at a time:

- Where or how will [insert stakeholder group name, e.g., customers] expect to receive the organization's communications and updates regarding a crisis?

- Is the appropriate team currently equipped to successfully achieve this means of communication?

- What are the next steps we need to take?

Let's run through some different means of communication that may apply to one or more of your stakeholder groups, along with some important aspects that should be considered for effective and efficient communication dissemination.

Telephone

Some stakeholders may naturally pick up the phone to call the members of your team with whom they have relationships. If so:

- Which stakeholders will be most inclined to do this—and why? (It is always important to understand why things are a certain way, especially in crisis management!)

- What number(s) will they call?

- Should there be a dedicated hotline? If so, whom should it be for and how will you provide them with the hotline number? Who will be responsible for setting this up?

- How many calls do you anticipate, and do you have enough resources to handle the influx of calls?

- Will the people who answer these calls be equipped with the approved messaging?

- Have they been trained in their crisis management roles and responsibilities?

Furthermore, will some stakeholders expect the organization to pick up the phone and deliver the news to them personally? If so:

- Which stakeholders have this expectation?

- Is the expectation to receive a courtesy call, before receiving something more official, such as an email or snail mail? Or will they expect real-time phone calls for each new development? If so, is this realistically achievable?

- Who, within your team, is responsible for making these calls?

- Are the appropriate people equipped with all relevant contact information?

- What if systems were down, would they still have everything they need to execute on this task?

Email

When done right, email can be an effective and direct means of crisis communication, as the messages can be personalized and efficiently distributed. Furthermore, people can choose to opt-in to receive email updates when a crisis is ongoing, if you deem this a worthwhile strategy. The following questions will help you determine whether email is a strategic means of crisis communication for your organization:

- Which stakeholders will expect to receive email notifications and updates from the organization?

- Who will be responsible for sending these emails?

- Are these team members equipped with all relevant contact information and / or do they have access to the appropriate email distribution programs?

- Should you develop an email template? For example, should you add a crisis template within your email distribution service, such as MailChimp, Aweber, or Infusionsoft?

- Should you provide an email opt-in option for stakeholders to subscribe to receive notifications and updates throughout the management of the crisis?

- What if your systems are down? Do you have an alternative means to still execute on this task and meet these expectations?

- Are there specific scenarios or times where an email notification (or other form of written notification) is required by law?

- If so, when and whom do these requirements apply to? For example, depending on the jurisdictions of impact, there will be legally required written notifications to send to impacted parties of certain types of cybersecurity incidents.

Website

I'm a firm advocate for designating your corporate website—or its equivalent—as your dedicated crisis communication hub. When used strategically, your website can help you extend the reach of your crisis communications and position your organization as the authoritative source of information. It's real estate that your organization owns and has full control over, which today is more of a rarity than a commonality. In order to effectively leverage your website as a crisis communication platform, start by answering the following questions:

- Which of your stakeholders will instinctively navigate to your corporate website for news and updates regarding the crisis?

- When they arrive to your website, what is the easiest way for them to find what they are looking for? For example, does it make sense to have a banner at the top of the homepage—or on strategic landing pages—that addresses the crisis and funnels people to the appropriate section of the website where they can find your published communications?

- If so, during what types of crises would this be helpful versus other types of crises, or levels of crises, where it may be overkill?

- Where will you publish your approved crisis communications? You should have a clearly defined designated location, such as your corporate blog, your newsroom, or a dark section within your website that activates in the event of a crisis. (I'll go further into the dark section concept later on in this chapter.)

- How will you publish your crisis communications and updates? For example, will each update be a new page or post? If so, will previous updates be as easy to find as the newer ones?

- How will you organize your crisis communications for ease of use? For example, you don't want to bury your crisis communications so deep within your website that they're not intuitively found, nor do you want to publish them in the form of a .pdf. (Please, please, please don't do this one!)

- Have you trained the right people in publishing new content to the appropriate location within your website? You want to cut out any middle people as much as possible, so if you currently rely on a third party to publish any new content to your website, you should consider integrating a content management system within your website and training the right people internally to be able to publish when the time comes.

- How will you help your team optimize your crisis communications for maximum reach and findability? Search engine optimization, so that people can find your statements in a Google search, and site-wide search capabilities are two good places to start.

Intranet or password protected portal

If you have an internal website that you regularly use to communicate with employees, or if you have some form of external password protected website or portal that you use to communicate with external stakeholders, make use of it if stakeholders will instinctively navigate there. When exploring these options, consider the following:

- How will these platforms be used, and by whom, in the event of a crisis?

- What will stakeholders expect to find when navigating to these platforms?

- Are there particular features or functions that stakeholders will expect to use (for example, a forum or messaging feature) or are these platforms set up with special features or functions that may prove helpful to your crisis communication efforts?

- Are there specific features or functions that these platforms do not currently have that you should consider adding or implementing, as they would be beneficial to the organization in times of crisis?

- What alternative means of communication would you use to achieve the same objectives, in the event that systems are down and you cannot access or use these platforms?

Face-to-face communication

Face-to-face communication can take many forms, from press conferences to recorded video messages published online. There are times when this type of communication strategy will be effective and beneficial, and other times when it can hinder your crisis management success. Therefore, when determining when and what shape this type of communication strategy may take, following are some things to consider:

- In what types of crises, and at what point within their management, would it be to your advantage to communicate in a face-to-face manner? Why and with whom?

- In what types of situations would your stakeholders expect some form of in-person communication? For example, in the event of an onsite accident that disrupts the community or the environment, community members may expect a town hall meeting to voice their concerns and gain answers to their questions. In this type of situation, when and how would you conduct this type of in-person meeting?

- What will be your ultimate goals and objectives in this form of communication?

- What form will this face-to-face communication take? For example, will it be a press conference, a town hall meeting, a video conference, a video recording published online, a livestream, etc.?

- Who will be responsible for each of these live communications? Have they been adequately trained? This includes everybody from the person who will be speaking with stakeholders to the people setting up behind the scenes and insuring attendance, and everything in between.

- Are there additional ways to leverage technology to extend the reach of these live communications? For example, could they be live-streamed or recorded and then published online?

- Who will be responsible for the technological side of the execution of this communication strategy?

Social media / mobile technology

Social media platforms and mobile technology can be great for helping you extend the reach and visibility of your crisis communications, and for helping you communicate with your key stakeholders on their turf. When determining when and how social media and mobile technology will be beneficial to your crisis communications, consider the following:

- What apps and / or social media platforms do your different stakeholders currently use to communicate with, or follow the communications of, your organization?

- Are there specific apps, social media platforms, or any other form of technology that your key stakeholders use in their daily lives that may present an opportunity to help you streamline your crisis communications directly to them?

- Do these platforms have special features or functions that you should be sure to incorporate into your dissemination processes? For example, when leveraging platforms such as Twitter and Instagram, you should absolutely incorporate a hashtag strategy into your messaging and dissemination. What are some other features and functions that you should incorporate?

- In times of crisis, what is the best way to use these platforms? Should you republish the entirety of your crisis communications to them, or should you simply use them to disseminate specific key message points, followed by a call to action that brings people back to your website or other main platform(s) for more information? Should they be a part of your primary means of communication, or your secondary?

- How is your team prepared to monitor and engage on these platforms, in real time, throughout the management of a crisis?

The Press Release

I face a lot of resistance with this one, but the fact is, when it comes to your in-crisis communications, the press release is dead. Let me explain.

The press release used to be a great way for organizations to get the word out in times of crisis. They would create a brief and formal communication, send it out on the wires, and hope the media ran with it. Today, organizations have far more effective and advantageous ways to communicate on their own terms. With the use of your website, social media, and other technologies, your organization has the opportunity to own its story and be its own publisher. You no longer have to wait and hope that the media picks up your message and tells your side of the story. Instead, you can and should take charge and take control!

Furthermore, the press release relies on a very stiff written format. Best practice dictates that press releases be short, in the third-person, and very formal. But that's not necessarily the best way to communicate with your stakeholders. As we have already discussed, you want to communicate in a way that is emotionally relatable, compassionate, and personable. The press release is not the best way to achieve this.

Whenever I make this statement, I regularly come up against the same three arguments:

1. The media still monitors the news wires;

2. The media needs the information to be short and concise, as they don't have time to sift through lengthy communications; and

3. The press release includes necessary media contact information.

Let's examine each argument:

1. Yes, the media still monitors the news wires, but they also monitor Twitter and other platforms, which are already a part of your crisis communication strategy. Additionally, your media relations team members maintain relationships with members of the media that regularly report on your industry and organization. Therefore, part of their crisis management roles and responsibilities will include reaching out to these contacts directly, to provide them with a courtesy heads-up. This is a far better strategy, for multiple reasons, than issuing a press release.

   As for the remaining members of the media that will report on the crisis, if you're effectively communicating while the crisis is being managed, then they will quickly and easily find those communications via your website, social media, or live broadcasts. In this day and age, we don't need to rely on the news wires to distribute our communications to this stakeholder group.

2. Yes, it's true that the media wants the information you provide to be short and concise. But so do your other stakeholders. No one wants to read tons of unnecessary information; they just want

When it comes to in-crisis communication, the press release is dead.

to find the pieces that are relevant to them. Therefore, this concept should be incorporated into all your crisis communication strategies and messaging. You want to be thorough and informative, but you also don't want to say more than you need to.

3. Press releases are not the only way to provide the media with relevant contact information. For some reason, I want to say "duh" here! Whichever location you choose to designate as your crisis communicate hub or home base should also include *all* relevant contact information for all stakeholder groups. For example, include the appropriate media relations contact information so that the media can reach out with additional questions and concerns, just as you should include the contact information of any other team members that specific stakeholder groups may want to reach out to, for the same reasons.

In times of crisis, your communications team will have a lot on their plate, so avoiding redundancy is appreciated. The press release is a redundancy. That said, if you still choose to use one as part of your crisis communication dissemination process, make sure it is a secondary means of communication, rather than primary. Your primary should really be on digital real estate that you own and control, such as your website.

With all of that said, an interesting way to use a press release is after a crisis. In this context, a press release can summarize events and their management, and announce their conclusion, letting people know that business operations have resumed to normal capacity.

However, a valid exception to this "the press release is dead for in-crisis communications" rule is if no other form of public communication is recognized legally by regulatory requirements. This is a very rare rule that is quickly going extinct. However, for the time being, it may still apply in some cases.

For example, if yours is a public company and your CEO passes away, securities law dictates that this is material information for certain stakeholders, such as investors and the general public. While we can argue that publishing the announcement to your corporate website will achieve the same results, your legal department may advise you to issue a press release to minimize potential risk, as the press release may still be the most accepted means of distribution for this type of material information...at least for the time being.

This is another important reason why working closely with different members of your team, including members of your legal and compliance departments, is incredibly important. You need to understand all realities, impacts, and risks before solidifying your crisis management strategies.

The dark section strategy

Earlier, I mentioned implementing a "dark section" within your website, as part of your crisis communication home base. It's time to look at what this means and how it works, but before we do, I want to be clear: maybe developing a dark section into your corporate website makes sense for your crisis preparedness, and maybe it doesn't. What are important are the fundamentals of this type of strategy, and how you can implement these fundamentals in many ways. Understand the basic principles and determine the best way to leverage them and make them work for your organization.

A dark section is a crisis communication home base, developed in a designated section of your website that is activated only in the event of a crisis. You may be familiar with a similar strategy: developing a dark *website*. However, it is rare that a dark website is the right crisis communication strategy to take. Why? Because a dark website is not intuitive to your stakeholders, since they don't know it exists prior to it being activated.

A dark website is published on its own domain at the onset of a crisis, so it does not have effective SEO standards. This means that your crisis communications will not have any advantage in search engine rankings. Dark websites also get "turned off" or unpublished once the crisis has been resolved, which means that all the organization's crisis communications and updates are removed from the internet. This doesn't serve your best interest. While it may be a welcome thought to get rid of all evidence of the crisis once it's resolved, what happens when future customers, clients, investors, employees, or the media learn about the crisis and want to do their own research? What conclusions will they draw when they can't find your organization's brilliant and effective communications?

For these reasons, dark *sections* are more useful in a crisis context. Not only is a dark section not hampered by these disadvantages, it also enables you to have a designated area to publish your crisis communications and updates. However, if your corporate website already has a blog or newsroom, it can serve this same advantage, without needing the additional work that a dark section requires to be developed.

The real advantage of implementing a dark section is that it enables you to strategize and be well prepared with everything you will need in the event of a crisis. For example, earlier we mentioned including all relevant contact information. This is something that can be done ahead of time, and activated in the heat of the moment.

Following is an example of a crisis dark section strategy that I developed and oversaw the implementation of for a client. While this was the right strategy for this particular client, depending on your current setup and needs you may be able to implement the fundamentals of this strategy *without* developing a designated dark section.

Concept to Reality

I have a client that has two websites: their main corporate website, and a designated newsroom website that serves as a corporate blog and media-specific publication platform. Each of these websites has its own URL. The newsroom website is updated regularly and serves as the organization's communication platform for customers, the media, and other key stakeholders. Since stakeholders already use this platform, it made sense to designate it as the organization's home base in the event of a crisis.

However, this savvy organization wanted to be more prepared than that. They wanted more than to merely use the platform to publish news and updates. They wanted a specialized location that would serve their crisis communication needs in a strategic way. Here is what we did:

Using the newsroom regularly as a marketing and communications tactic meant much of the content was irrelevant in times of crisis. Therefore, on the backend of this newsroom, a toggle was developed. When clicked, this toggle removes all content that is irrelevant to the crisis from the frontend of the newsroom, and replaces it with a new navigation system (i.e., menu) and a subtle, branded design. The layout of this dark section was developed to display all updates and communications that the organization publishes throughout the management of a crisis clearly and concisely. We also implemented some key components, such as contact information, site-wide messaging, and an email alert opt-in to be leveraged as needed.

The whole point of this dark section is simply to make it easy and efficient for the organization to position itself as the narrative of their own crisis right from the start, and to provide key stakeholders with a dedicated and intuitive platform to rely on for regular updates concerning the crisis and its management.

Post-crisis, we developed a simple way for the crisis communications team to index all published crisis communications, making them findable in the future even after the toggle is switched back and the newsroom returns to its normal everyday use.

This dark section serves this particular organization's crisis communication needs. It also gives them the advantage of choosing to leverage this function in the event of a significant crisis, while having the flexibility to simply use their regular newsroom in times of issue management or crises that call for a less dramatic approach.

Developing a dark section within your corporate website may or may not be the right strategy for your crisis management needs. Now that you are armed with this knowledge, you're in a position to execute the best strategy for your organization.

There are multiple ways to communicate with your key stakeholders in times of crisis. It is up to you to determine the most strategic and efficient ways, depending on the crisis scenario and the stakeholder group. When developing these dissemination strategies, don't forget to determine the primary versus secondary means of communication for each of your stakeholder groups. For example, in some high-risk scenarios, the primary means of communication may be sending an email and publishing to your digital home base, whereas other high-risk scenarios may involve picking up the phone first and following that conversation up with an email.

Once you have your strategy of response determined, the next step is to begin drafting the main message points for your crisis communication handbook. However, before we dive into drafting this messaging, I want to take a moment to address a few frequently asked questions.

SHOULD ALL STAKEHOLDERS GET THE SAME INFORMATION?

Yes, as long as it's pertinent to them. There is a common misconception that employees should be provided with more information than external stakeholders are. While this may be true for a select group of individuals, such as managers and directors, it is not true for the entire company population. Why? Because messaging should be consistent across the board.

What happens if you provide additional information to employees and it is leaked or accidentally shared with investors or the media? You can't take it back and it may hinder or complicate your crisis management. Therefore, consistency is paramount.

You should still be aware, however, of your different stakeholder groups. They may have different concerns or questions, depending on what the crisis means to them. In this regard, it makes sense for you to address specific concerns with one stakeholder group while addressing different concerns with another. Nevertheless, your key message points need to remain consistent, no matter to whom you are speaking.

Oftentimes, this employee communication misconception stems from a good place. Employees want to feel as though they are valued and trusted members of the team, and they deserve as much. This is a great objective to have and one way to accomplish this is to communicate with employees *first*, if you have the time to do so. While your messaging will remain consistent, the act of prioritizing their communications can be a great way to display your appreciation of your team and make them feel included. This actually leads me to the next commonly posed question I receive...

WHAT IS THE ORDER OF YOUR COMMUNICATIONS?

Internally, you want to prioritize the dissemination of your communications in order to make sure managers and directors are aware of the situation and have the necessary talking points. In other words, you don't want employees asking their managers questions that they are unprepared to answer—or worse, catching them completely off guard. Develop this feature into your internal dissemination processes and protocols.

Apart from that, however, whom you communicate with and when depends on a number of things that should be incorporated into your crisis communication strategy, depending on the scenario and its specificities. Consider, for example:

The emergency level of the crisis

In the event of an emergency crisis, where people's lives or safety may be in jeopardy, clearly prioritize communication with them before anyone else. This can include scenarios such as a natural disaster and workplace violence.

Those directly impacted

If a crisis affects your organization's ability to perform, produce, or deliver, then customers and clients would certainly prefer to hear this news from you before they hear about it from a third party, such as the media.

Stakeholder expectations

Are there scenarios where certain stakeholders will expect to receive a courtesy heads-up prior to you going public with your communications? Additionally, as we saw in chapter three, you may have different tiers of stakeholders, within your different stakeholder groups, that will expect and / or require prioritized communication.

Legal or regulatory requirements

Are there certain scenarios where you are required by law or regulation to prioritize certain communications and notifications?

The luxury of time

Do you have it? For example, does timing permit you the opportunity to provide employees with a compassionate and live notification of the incident, and can you do this before the story begins going viral and you lose all control over the narrative?

It all boils down to two things:

1. Doing the right thing, such as prioritizing people's safety and well-being; and

2. Valuing and maintaining the trusting relationships you share with your stakeholders.

Use these two important objectives as a guiding beacon when answering this question for each of your high-risk scenarios. In fact, use these two important objectives as a guiding beacon in all aspects of your crisis management and crisis communication. If you have a handle on these points, you are well on your way to a crisis ready culture already.

IT'S TIME TO START DRAFTING!

After developing the internal and external processes and strategies for communicating with each key stakeholder, the time has come to develop scenario-specific crisis communication handbooks. These handbooks will include strategies of response and preliminarily drafted messaging. Whenever you are ready, turn the page and let's start developing these together!

CREATING YOUR CRISIS COMMUNICATION HANDBOOKS

To remain consistent with chapter six, we are going to develop your crisis communication handbook for a cybersecurity incident. While we do this, I want you to keep the following two things in mind:

1. There is no one-size-fits-all answer or strategy. This is why I will always give you the reasoning for a decision or approach. It is important for you to understand the *why* and then use that to develop a tailored and practical communication handbook for your organization; and

2. We cannot possibly cover every aspect of your crisis preparedness within these pages. For this reason, it's important to work closely with the experts on your team who specialize in unique areas of expertise. Their input, viewpoints, and prowess will compliment yours, along with the information shared throughout the pages of this book and, together, you will develop a solid program that will be ready to be tested.

As I mentioned, you want your handbooks to be as short and concise as possible. Anything that is not needed for the purpose of clarity or practicality in the midst of a crisis doesn't belong in your handbook. Additionally, I also like to keep the layout and structure of each handbook consistent for ease of use and reference. With that said, let's develop your handbook for a cybersecurity event, section by section. Adapt the following information and concepts to fit your organization's needs.

SECTION 1: CRISIS RESPONSE OVERVIEW

The purpose of this section is to provide all necessary information regarding the scenario and the organization's strategy of response in a simple and concise manner. Try to keep this section no more than two to three pages. Developing the following components first will also help guide your message drafting for section two.

Scenario definition

Briefly define the scenario and describe at what point the scenario becomes a corporate crisis and therefore, at what point this handbook comes into play. This can go one of two ways:

1. Incorporate the criteria we discussed in chapter four, when we defined the difference between an issue and a crisis.

2. Include a line that says something like: This handbook is to be activated upon declaration of a corporate crisis by [insert name for leadership team].

Scenario categorization

This section does not apply to all scenarios. If this is the case, leave it out. However, one common scenario it *does* apply to is a cybersecurity crisis. (Huh, funny how that worked out!) To determine if your high-risk scenarios have different categories of events, you want to think about the different ways the scenario can occur and determine whether those different ways will change or influence your response and messaging.

Following are three categories that exist within the cybersecurity crisis theme.

1. A calculated attack against the organization. This type of breach happens due to malicious intent.

2. A human or operational error that results in the organization suffering a breach. In this category, there is no malicious intent, simply error.

3. A third party suffers a breach and, unfortunately, your data or systems get breached or impacted as a result.

The tone of your crisis communications will differ slightly depending on these categories. For example, if a breach happens because of a calculated, malicious attack against your organization, the tone of your communications will be different than if you had to explain that your vendor suffered a breach and, as a result, your internal systems were impacted.

Another trick I've learned is to make these categories of events more tangible by including some real-world examples in the description, such as malware and social engineering examples. The lines can get blurry when we start looking at categories of events within a given scenario, and it can quickly become confusing. Therefore, you want to be clear that the focus is solely on "when might the tone of our messaging be different?" and then make this real for others by including examples. Define these categories, and their examples, with the use of a simple table for easy reference.

Goals and objectives

In bullet point form, clearly define what the organization's crisis communications goals and objectives are. We discussed this at the start of this chapter, so feel free to go back a few pages, leverage what we discussed, and tailor them to the specifics of the scenario.

Strategy by stakeholder group

Here, you want to provide an at-a-glance outline of the predetermined strategy you will use when communicating with each of your key stakeholder groups. It is possible that some situations demand you be proactive with certain stakeholders and reactive with others. For example, in the event that employee PII is breached because of a third party hack, you will need to proactively communicate with employees to let them know what happened, how it happened, what you are doing about it, and how they can protect themselves from identify theft. However, you aren't going to call customers to let them know that your employees' PII was compromised due to your bank suffering a breach. Instead, when it comes to customers and other relevant stakeholders, you should be more reactive. This way, you will be ready to answer their questions and calm their concerns in the event that they have any.

It is important that you think through and clearly define what your communications approach will be in different scenarios. When will you be reactive versus proactive, and with whom, and when might that direction change? What will be your primary versus secondary means of communication, and why? Display this information in a simple way in order to be clear and concise, and for the team to instantly comprehend the strategy at a quick glance.

SECTION 2: DRAFT CRISIS COMMUNICATIONS

This is the meat of your handbook. If you have several categories of events, then break this section up by category and make sure you are adequately prepared for the different directions and tones that apply.

Remember that these are preliminary communications that will need to be finalized in the midst of a crisis. You should never just blindly use what you have drafted. Ever. These are templates for messaging. You will need to insert particular details later, when needed. Prior to experiencing a crisis, you have the luxury of time and thoughtful contemplation; take this time to develop communications that will give your team a head start in a crisis. Take this time to ensure alignment on messaging and strategy of response with all appropriate members of your team.

First response or holding statement

As we discussed in chapters two and three, time is of the essence in a crisis and the sooner you communicate appropriately, the better. Your first response lets stakeholders know that you are aware of the incident, what you are doing about it, and that they can rely on you for real-time updates. When done correctly, your first response statement establishes your organization as the credible source of information throughout the crisis while buying you time to gather and confirm facts.

However, there's a catch! Stakeholders expect much more from a first response statement today than they have in the past. Organizations that don't realize this end up suffering unnecessary criticism, as they come across as cagey and opaque. Case in point: the example we saw earlier with United Airlines when they attempted to put out a minimalistic statement when their CEO suffered a heart attack. Not only was this statement reactionary when it should have been proactive (they waited until the media started reporting on the facts and their stock price began taking a hit), but their messaging did everything but satisfy stakeholders' questions and concerns.

When it comes to your first response statement, you need to remember a few key points. First, it is okay to not have all the information as long as you don't avoid the obvious or what is expected. Second, there is a delicate balance between saying the right amount and not saying enough (like United) or saying too much (like Samsung). So, how do you draft a first response statement that hits all the right marks? Here are some pointers:

- Let stakeholders know that you are aware of the incident, or that an incident has occurred. If you are the first to announce that the incident happened, be sure to work closely with legal and other team members to determine the right time to make this announcement. You ideally want to get ahead of the story, but you also don't want to speak too soon and put the organization at legal or other risk. Look at all circumstances, risks and benefits when making this decision. Some situations are more obvious and black and white then others.

- State what you know for sure, at a given moment. What you say in this statement depends on what you are able to say, but you can always say something. In a crisis, there is no excuse for no comment.

- Describe what you are doing, in some detail. For example, instead of saying, "we're investigating the situation", say something like, "we're in the process of working closely with forensic specialists and law enforcement to determine the full extent of the breach and to identify its root cause."

- Eliminate the elephant from the room. If there are key concerns that you know stakeholders will have, address them. Even if you don't have the answers, let them know that you are aware of their concerns and that acquiring the answers is a priority to you.

- Be compassionate, personable, and emotionally intelligent.

- Your first response statement should be long enough to say everything you can and should say, though short enough that you don't end up putting your foot in your mouth.

- Let people know that you will be committed to providing timely updates as you confirm information. If stakeholders feel as though they can trust the organization to be forthright and transparent, then they probably won't feel a need to go to a third party for news and updates.

- Provide links or directives as to where they can find these updates.

- Provide relevant contact information.

Some tips on what *not* to do:

- Don't be ambiguous. This will frustrate stakeholders and result in unnecessary criticism and questions.

- Don't speak in legal or industry jargon. Speak in human.

- Don't avoid the obvious. (Remember that elephant!)

- Don't avoid the facts, unless you have legal reasons for doing so. If you are prohibited from providing certain pieces of information, let them know so they can understand what your situation is and assure them that you will provide them with the answers to their questions as soon as you are able.

Example cybersecurity first response statement

Cybersecurity incidents are not black-and-white scenarios. Sometimes you know you have been breached, but the investigation can take months before you have more information. Maybe you will have the luxury of time to conduct the needed investigation before word gets out, and maybe you won't. Maybe laws and regulations will require you to communicate sooner than is comfortable, and maybe they won't. Other times, you may find out from law enforcement that you've been breached, and this news may prohibit you from communicating, as you'll risk hindering their bigger investigation into catching the culprit. So, while you can identify the different types of events and ways that a cybersecurity incident may come to be your reality, you can never know the conditions under which it will unfold until you're faced with the situation.

Therefore, when pre-drafting a first response or holding statement for this type of high-risk scenario, I usually design it to be used in the following conditions.

In the event that news regarding the situation has been leaked, people are expecting information, and:

- The organization has confirmed there has been a breach and an investigation is underway, though no further information has yet been confirmed; or

- The authorities have prohibited communication regarding the manner; or

- An investigation confirmed that the breach has been contained and eradicated, and no data or systems have been compromised (meaning it is not a crisis).

Here's what this holding statement might look like:

[Insert appropriate salutations],

[We are writing to notify you that] on [date], our IT department detected [insert high-level details of situation].

Company has always prioritized information security and, as such, we continuously strive to implement and maintain cybersecurity best practices. [We do this by [insert high-level details, if appropriate]].

[Upon detection, our team quickly contained the threat and conducted a thorough forensics investigation. We are happy to report that the investigation has left us with no reason to believe that our data or systems have been compromised. As a result, our team continues to operate their daily activities as usual].

OR

[Upon detection, our team immediately worked to contain the threat, activated our cybersecurity incident response plan, and informed the proper authorities. Our top priority at this time is [insert high-level details of ongoing actions and commitments, e.g., working closely with forensic specialists and law enforcement to determine the full extent of the incident]].

[What we have confirmed at this point in time is [insert confirmed facts that can be shared]].

[Protecting our [insert terms for stakeholders, e.g., customers', partners', etc.] [data / information] is our top priority].

[Our team will be committed to keeping you informed, [if / as] new developments arise. Any new developments and updates will be published to [insert link to crisis communication home base]].

OR

[As our investigation ensues, and as new developments get confirmed, we will be committed to providing you with updates. All new developments and updates will be published to [insert link to crisis communication home base]].

[Furthermore, our dedicated team will be in direct communication with any impacted parties to provide them with ongoing information and support].

If you have any questions or concerns at any time, please don't hesitate to reach out to [insert appropriate contact information].

[To learn more about *Company*'s commitment to cybersecurity, click here [insert appropriate link]].

Sincerely,

[Sign appropriately]

* Brackets mean that the content is optional and / or needs to be completed with specific information.

This example first response statement is very corporate-sounding. It is also very generic for the purpose of this book. If your organization's tone is usually very corporate, then the tone of this sample messaging will probably fall in line with the tone of your crisis communications. However, remember that it is important to come across as a caring organization that is committed to righting this wrong, no matter how corporate your brand's tone may be. On the other hand, if your brand has a more distinct tone, then you want to remain in line with that branding—but be careful! You want stakeholders to recognize the brand that they have grown to know, while also keeping in mind that you are communicating an important message that people care about, especially because it may affect them in a negative way. Be mindful of your branding, and be mindful of the emotions that your stakeholders will feel. The last thing you want is to come across as insensitive, so pay attention to how your communications validate those emotions.

The official response statement

The first response statement buys you the time you need when you aren't yet ready to provide the necessary details. Once you have confirmed more information, issue a more complete statement with this information. In some situations, you may or may not need the first response statement; but you will always need to come out with an official response statement, along with any subsequent updates.

This is when you really start to provide confirmed answers to pertinent questions and concerns, keeping key stakeholders current on new developments. This is also where you continue to demonstrate that you are a true leader, worthy of your stakeholders' trust, support, and loyalty—and forgiveness, in some cases.

The official response statement section of your handbook is where your messaging will meet the need to communicate effectively in each of the different categories you identified earlier. For example, if we follow suit with the three categories we identified for a cybersecurity incident, this section of your handbook will contain official response statements for each of these three categories. The core structure of the messaging will be consistent across all categories, though there will be nuanced differences in language and tone.

Depending on the structure of your crisis communication processes and protocols, you may choose to draft anything from main message points to full-length templates of messaging for individual stakeholder groups. For example, if your communications department is responsible for drafting all the organization's crisis communications before disseminating them to the appropriate stakeholder owners, then this section may include drafted main message points, full-length notifications for each stakeholder group, and a draft of the dissemination email. However, if your crisis communication protocols and processes dictate that stakeholder owners are responsible for drafting their own full-length notifications with the approved message points, then this section will only include drafted main message points, along with the drafted email for dissemination.

The goal is to provide your team with a head start in drafting and finalizing your crisis communications when time is of the essence. The way you go about doing this will depend on your governance structure and the processes you have developed up until this point.

Additionally, as your official response statement and all subsequent updates should be as informative as possible, do you remember those "key anticipated questions" I had you think through and draft earlier in this chapter? Well, this is where those come in. When drafting your main message points, draft answers to the anticipated questions you're able to answer at this point in time. From there, you will continue to let those pertinent questions guide you as the team conducts its investigations and gathers the facts in the heat of the moment.

As you confirm new information and get answers to pertinent questions, communicate! If the crisis is long-lasting (like an oil spill that will take weeks or months to clean up) you should consider developing a structured timeline for all subsequent updates. For example, can you promise an update every evening, in which you can report on the day's progress and communicate new developments and confirmed facts? If so, then this will go a long way towards providing consistency and demonstrating your commitment to keeping stakeholders informed.

Supplemental messaging

Supplemental messaging is any communication that you can foresee needing that is either not applicable in all circumstances, or for every stakeholder group. Your supplemental messaging can be drafted as small paragraphs or bulleted message points. Some possible communications to draft for this section include:

- Employee-specific directives to be incorporated into your internal crisis communications as needed. This may include messaging such as: "In accordance with *Company*'s social media policy, please do not post, publish, or communicate on social media regarding this incident. We have a dedicated team monitoring and responding on social media to ensure that all of our communications are consistent and factual. If you receive inquiries on social media or notice any comments that should be addressed or monitored, please forward them to [insert appropriate team's contact information]."

- Fact sheets that provide necessary information concerning a specific scenario. For example, if you work in an industry that deals with hazardous material and one of your high-risk scenarios is a spill, explosion, or a leak, your team will benefit from a fact sheet that provides them with important information concerning possible effects on people and / or the environment.

- Redirect banners to publish to the top of appropriate website landing pages—for example, banners that funnel viewers to your designated home base.

- Anything else that may seem relevant and helpful in different types of situations.

Questions to anticipate

We have discussed the need to identify and anticipate the most pertinent questions that each of your stakeholders will have for each high-risk scenario. This section will house these questions. Whether you choose to list them as simple bullet points or a full-blown FAQ, develop these as much as you are able to prior to the crisis striking—and don't forget to reference them while in the midst of a crisis!

Translation

If your organization operates in different regions, or if it caters to different cultures or stakeholders that speak different languages, then you will want to have your drafted communications translated as appropriate.

And there you have it!

I warned you that it was going to be a lot of work, but I hope you can see how helpful having all of these elements and strategies prepared in advance is to your team. How detailed you choose to be in your crisis communication handbooks depends on your organization and its high-risk scenarios. Remember, though, to keep each handbook as short and concise as possible.

If you have done all the exercises shared in this book, you officially have your crisis ready program's foundation, as well as your first playbook and communication handbook drafted. Congratulations!

There is one last element of your crisis ready program that I want to address: your *post*-crisis preparedness. As you'll see in the next chapter, the crisis rarely ends once it has been managed. Since you've already put all this work into being crisis ready, let's go the last mile. It's time to give you what you need to ensure that after a crisis, your team will be able to mitigate lingering risk and reestablish your business status quo.

08

THE DAY AFTER TOMORROW

In the evening of April 20, 2010, 4.9 million barrels of oil began spewing into the Gulf of Mexico when BP's offshore drilling rig exploded. This oil spill, which surged for eighty-seven days and is the largest marine oil spill in history, killed eleven people onboard the rig.

The crisis wasn't over even after the spill was under control and the reporters had gone home. In fact, it was not even close to being over. It took three years of cleanup, more than $18 billion[30] in settlements and fines, and approximately 3,000 civil lawsuits in both U.S. and foreign courts before BP finally began to put this monumental crisis behind them. Then, in 2016, Hollywood released *Deepwater Horizon*, a movie directed by Peter Berg and starring Mark Wahlberg, Kurt Russell, and Kate Hudson, bringing the story back to the forefront of everyone's minds once again. This time, the narrative highlighted the human tragedy and corporate corruption that took place aboard the rig.

> Similar to the Wells Fargo scandal, the CRP is difficult to calculate for this crisis, as the repercussions were a result of the magnitude of the incident and its impact. However, we *can* talk about the soft CRP. When you think about BP today, how do you feel? Does your mind instantly associate the company's name with the Gulf of Mexico oil spill? What about when you hear the quote, "I'd like my life back"? Do you immediately conjure images of BP's former CEO, Tony Hayward, and the sentiment of this thoughtless comment? If, like countless others, you answered "yes" to any of these questions, then you just experienced firsthand the long-lasting impact of the soft CRP that this disastrous crisis, and its management caused for BP.

A crisis rarely ends when leadership disbands the crisis team and reports that it is back to business as usual. Far too often, the organization must pick up the pieces of a broken reputation; navigate through a loss of revenue, profits, and / or an impact on stock price; suffer through prolonged litigation; and potentially need to shrink the organization, which can mean budget cuts, layoffs, and more.

The day after tomorrow can be even more impactful and long-lasting than the days of the crisis itself. Therefore, it is just as important to be *post-crisis* ready as it is to be crisis ready. In fact, if you are not post-crisis ready, you aren't fully crisis ready. So, how do you prepare for the day after tomorrow when tomorrow has not happened yet?

Just like every other aspect of your crisis ready program, you prepare by having the right conversations with the right people and by using those discussions to create a post-crisis review action plan for each of your high-risk scenarios. This post-crisis review action plan will sit towards the back of its respective playbook and will be developed to help guide the team through the right processes when the time comes. This is the last step in completing the development of your crisis ready program.

THE POST-CRISIS REVIEW

Your goal is going to be to develop an action plan or task consideration list that will help you effectively review and analyze the crisis and its management, as well as help you develop your post-crisis strategy and identify next steps. During the post-crisis review, your team will evaluate and discuss the following:

The actual incident
This includes fully understanding what happened, why it happened, and how to ensure that it—or a similar incident—never happens again.

Strategic next steps
What are the short- and long-term impacts of the crisis on the organization? What actions need to be taken to recover from any damages incurred, as well as mitigate any further damage or disruption?

The program and your team
Was the program helpful? Did you uncover any gaps or kinks that need to be amended? What about your team, how did they fare? Might they benefit from any additional training?

The time to implement this action plan will be once the crisis has been resolved and the team resumes their regular business activities. Every pertinent member of the crisis team should partake in this process. You may also choose to include your business continuity team, if your organization has one and if they are not already a part of the crisis team.

Like every other aspect of your crisis preparedness, conducting a successful post-crisis review requires the right mindset and dedicated follow-through. You must walk into this session with an open mind, ready to hear some harsh and unpleasant realities and willing to commit to the right actions to succeed and improve moving forward.

Since we've been using the high-risk scenario of a cybersecurity incident throughout the development of your program, it only makes sense to continue along this path. So, let's get to drafting your cybersecurity post-crisis review action plan and close out your first high-risk scenario!

STRATEGIZING YOUR POST-CRISIS REVIEW

First, you will want to speak with the right team members to make sure you gather their insight and foresight when drafting your post-crisis review action plan. This should come as no surprise if you have gotten this far in the book! For efficiency, I usually build these questions into my scenario-specific conversations—the ones we discussed back in chapters five, six, and seven. Some questions you will want to ask during this segment of the conversation will include:

- What are the key considerations and likely post-crisis repercussions that need to be accounted for? E.g., potential litigation, long-term impact on reputation, prolonged investigations by the authorities or regulators, impact on employee morale, etc.

- What are some likely post-crisis action items that your team would be responsible for implementing or undertaking? How long do you estimate it will take to complete these action items?

- What new expectations or demands would key stakeholders have of the organization moving forward, post-crisis?

When drafting this action plan, focus on being suggestive in a way that inspires and provokes contemplation and discussion, rather than being too specific. While you understand the high-risk scenario, you cannot *precisely* know how this scenario will unfold or play out in its management. Therefore, you want to make sure that the team considers all relevant angles and impacts no matter the situation.

Following, I am going to walk you through the structure of the post-crisis review. Consider what you need to achieve and keep in mind these considerations so you can better achieve your goals. Use this information to develop a scalable post-crisis review action plan for each one of your high-risk scenarios.

UNDERSTANDING THE ROOT CAUSE

While tackling the crisis, you will have determined the root cause of the incident, or at least have initiated the investigation into the root cause. During your post-crisis review, it is important that you discuss the root cause with your crisis team. For example, it is not enough to say, "The breach happened as a result of an employee error." You need to better assess the circumstances around this employee error so that you can put measures in place to prevent a reoccurrence. It is not possible to move on to any other area of a post-crisis review without truly understanding the reasons the incident happened in the first place.

Some points of discussion might include:

- How did the employee error occur?

- Why did the employee error occur?

- Could it have been prevented?

- Do security protocols need to be tightened? What might this look like?

- Are there other ways to avoid this type of error, or something similar, from happening again?

- How long did it take to identify the error? Could it—or should it—have been detected earlier on?

- Would earlier detection have mitigated some of the impact?

> *The post-crisis review should not be a blame game. You will not get the results you need, nor will you initiate moving forward in a progressive manner, if this exercise revolves around pointing fingers or deflecting. Instead, speak matter-of-factly in the interest of progressive evolution, validate the team's opinions and feelings, and praise team members for their honesty and participation.*

ASSESSING THE IMPACT

After determining the root cause, it is time to assess the impact. What is the overall effect of the crisis on the organization, its stakeholders, and / or the environment? Are there repercussions that may continue to develop or unfold over time? How might these repercussions manifest, how will they be detected, and how should they be managed—and by whom?

Sometimes the damage is obvious—plummeting stock prices or falling sales, for example. However, at other times determining the damage requires a little more digging. I once had a client that did not see an immediate hit to their sales or reputation in the post-crisis stage. However, upon further investigation—which included reaching out to, surveying, and speaking directly with past, current, and prospective customers—we uncovered that stakeholder trust in the organization was on seriously shaky ground. In this particular case, customers no longer felt that the organization's stated values were truly an integral part of its culture. Those shared values had originally connected customers to the brand in an emotionally powerful way.

> **This investigation revealed a hidden, yet soon-to-be-impactful, soft CRP that we were then able to mitigate.**

Identifying this profound repercussion was critical for the organization's post-crisis success. But identifying it before it was too late required more than simply looking on the surface. It required some strategic excavation. Fortunately, once we understood the real impact, we were able to take ongoing initiatives to demonstrate and prove the organization's commitment to their core values, enabling the organization to strengthen the existing trust and rebuild broken trust over time.

Other examples may include a pending or future risk of litigation or regulatory issues; cost of cleanup; impact on business operations, etc. Assessing the damage of the crisis will require that each crisis team member and department conduct a thorough analysis in their respective areas of expertise. While the answers may take some time to uncover, you will want to do your best to answer this question as quickly as possible—for example, over the coming weeks. The sooner you understand the depth of the damage, the sooner you can choose to take the appropriate actions to mend the broken pieces.

SUSTAINING YOUR BUSINESS

Now that you understand the depths of the cause of the crisis and its impact, it is the organization's responsibility to learn and improve from the experience. Remember the proper crisis ready mindset we discussed in chapter one? The final "S" in "CRISIS" is for:

Sustaining your business and your brand's reputation by choosing to learn from mistakes and by committing to improvement and positive evolution. This means implementing corrective actions and behaviors to right wrongs and ensure such an incident never happens again. You will not be forgiven for making the same mistake twice, so don't.

The first step in sustaining your business is to prevent potential reoccurrences. I am not just talking about a reoccurrence of the exact same incident. I am talking categorically. For example, let's use the previous example of a breach occurring due to an employee error, and let's say that the employee error happened when an employee accidentally emailed the wrong attachment with confidential information to the wrong recipients. The corrective measures you may choose to put in place here may include things like:

- Improved regular cybersecurity trainings for personnel;

- Tighter controls around sending confidential information to outside parties; and

- Implementation of a pop-up verification notification that comes up each time an attachment is added to an email draft.

While these may be good preventative measures for the exact same type of incident, you should also take the time to identify other ways that employee error may result in a cybersecurity crisis and mitigate them as well. Think how foolish you would appear if you had to explain a second employee error-related cybersecurity incident.

 This time it wasn't due to an email mistake; it was the result of a phishing scam that our employee fell victim to, as he unwittingly answered the strange and intrusive questions he was being asked, divulging his access to our internal systems which contain all your confidential information. Sorry about that!"

Finding yourself in the same mess will cause you to lose all credibility and trust. So, don't. All of this goes back to the idea of culture and mindset. Do you have a *culture* that chooses to learn from its mistakes and do what is necessary to better connect and earn the trust and respect of your stakeholders? This is a big question—and there is only one right answer.

DEVELOPING YOUR MOVE-FORWARD STRATEGY

At this point, you will have determined the underlying issues that caused the crisis; you will have a solid understanding of its long-term impact, and you will have identified appropriate measures to prevent a reoccurrence. Your next task will be to develop your post-crisis strategy for minimizing further damage, rebuilding trust, and repairing reputational loss.

Here are some questions and considerations aimed at helping you develop your post-crisis strategy. Of course, the right questions, topics, and answers will be dependent on the particulars of the given situation, which means you want to be suggestive in your planning, as mentioned earlier.

Learn about real-world, post-crisis impacts that people rarely discuss: melissaagnes.com/ fortmcmurray

Do your employees need additional support?

This can include anything from operational support, such as hiring experts or upgrading your systems, straight through to physical, emotional, or monetary support. For example, in the event of a workplace violence crisis, people may be suffering from injuries, and even if they are not, the psychological impact can be dire and long-lasting.

What actions need to be undertaken to right the wrongs?

For example, in the event of a cybersecurity incident where personally identifiable information has been stolen, you will be legally obliged to provide specific notifications, guidance, and help to impacted stakeholders, depending on the jurisdictions of the impacted regions. What might this look like, and what are your next steps for complying with these requirements? What actions can you take to go above and beyond these requirements?

In the event of other types of high-risk scenarios, you may need to strategize things like compensation to impacted parties, cleanup to the environment or property, a change in supply chain processes or key vendors, and more.

Is there risk of litigation?

If so, what needs to be done to prepare for or mitigate this risk? Your legal and communication or PR teams will be helpful here. For example, what are the next steps for the legal team to take, and might they require help from other departments (such as internal audit or compliance) or external subject matter experts (such as your outside counsel)?

From a communications standpoint, do you need to share or disclose this information with specific stakeholders, such as your board or investors? Or is it most strategic to keep it quiet until further developments occur? At what point might you need to be forthcoming with your communications, and to whom? At what point might it garner attention from the media and other stakeholders, and what will be your strategy of response?

Is there an impact on trust and credibility?

If trust has been impacted, how will you proceed to rebuild / strengthen that trust with your key stakeholders? What actions are you committing to and how should those actions be communicated, demonstrated, and measured?

What questions or concerns will stakeholders express moving forward, and how will you arm your teams with the answers to those questions to ensure accuracy and consistency across departments, regions, and stakeholder groups? Will you publish an informative FAQ to your crisis communication home base that answers all relevant questions?

Additionally, should you make a big public gesture, or quietly focus on rebuilding your reputation and relationships with key stakeholders? Oftentimes after a crisis, organizations want to stay as low-key as possible, which is normal after suffering through a high-profile disaster. Sometimes this is the best course of action, and other times proactively engaging and proving your commitment to change is an even stronger strategy. This decision depends on the incident and cannot be made lightly. It will require lots of thought, consideration, risk assessment, and possibly hiring an outside expert that has experience with post-crisis recovery programs.

Does your online reputation need repairing?

Your online reputation *is* your reputation these days. After a crisis, it is very possible that the countless news articles, blog posts, reviews, and social media comments that were published about your organization and the incident will linger at the top of the search engine results pages for who knows how long. This negatively affects different areas of your business—unless you do something about it. This may require an aggressive content strategy. However, an aggressive content strategy may not be appropriate post-crisis. Repairing your online reputation may be tricky and will probably require outside guidance from experts who have vast experience and a proven track record.

EVALUATING AND EVOLVING THE PROGRAM

Once your post-crisis strategy is in motion, take the opportunity to evaluate the practicality of your entire program as well as your team's crisis management efforts. This means you should take the time to discuss the crisis, its management, and the practicality of the program with your crisis team.

Was the program practical? Were there any resources or tools missing that would have served the team well in the heat of the moment? How does each person feel after the crisis? What are some of the biggest lessons and takeaways they learned throughout this experience?

Once you have had this discussion, take the opportunity to update and strengthen your crisis ready program as needed. From there, your next step will be to conduct a crisis team training to walk everyone through these changes and to thank them for giving the organization their all through this difficult time. It is important not to forget to thank and appreciate your team!

As you can see, the post-crisis review is an important element within your crisis ready plan. Taking time now to put dedicated thought into your post-crisis efforts and considerations will serve your organization and team well moving forward.

And there you have it! You now have everything you need to develop a scalable crisis ready program. Once the hard work of designing your program is over with, it will be time for the fun part! This fun part involves testing your program to make sure it is practical and beginning to implement that crisis ready culture I keep talking about.

This is what the next chapter is all about. I am going to walk you through conducting an insightful, practical, and *awesomely fun* crisis simulation. The heavy lifting is officially over, so it is time to get excited about something new. Let's go!

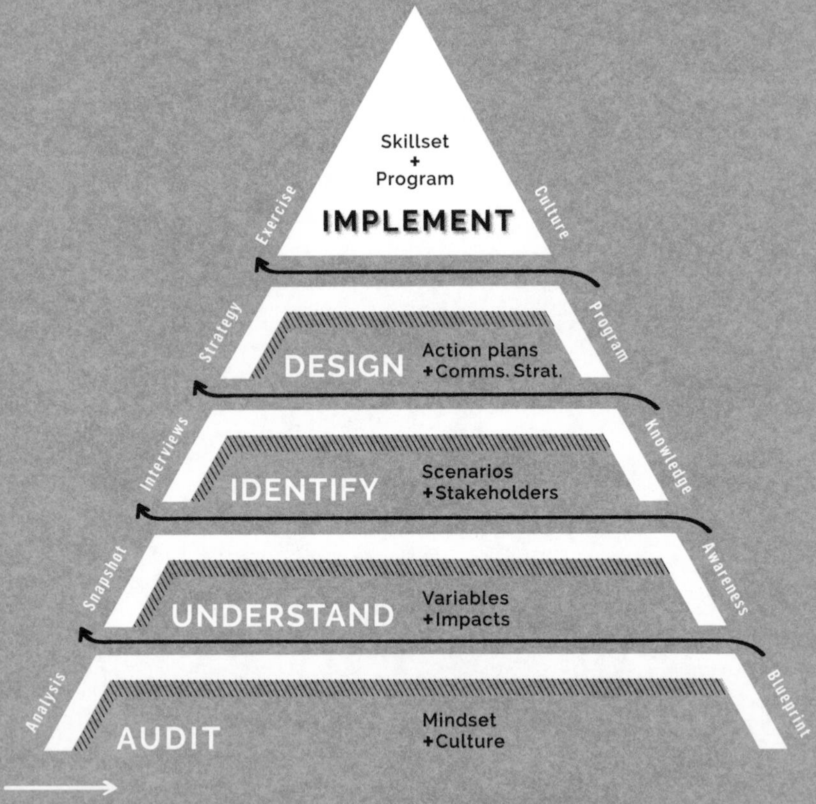
Skillset
+
Program
IMPLEMENT
Exercise
Culture
Strategy
Program
DESIGN
Action plans
+Comms. Strat.
Interviews
Knowledge
IDENTIFY
Scenarios
+Stakeholders
Snapshot
Awareness
UNDERSTAND
Variables
+Impacts
Analysis
Blueprint
AUDIT
Mindset
+Culture

09

SUCCESS IS A
DRESS REHEARSAL

It was a beautiful autumn morning and my team and I were excited about the day ahead. We had spent three months building an extremely realistic and dynamic crisis scenario for one of our most crisis ready clients. This client is in the energy business, and they take their crisis preparedness to a whole other level. They live and breathe a crisis ready culture. They have a mindset that looks for opportunity within risk, even before risk manifests. They have a savvy team that they train well, trust, and empower to make smart decisions that align with the organization's values and objectives. They have a crisis ready program that was developed years ago (long before this client became ours) and they work continuously to strengthen and improve it. In other words, this company is filled with our kind of people!

So, when my team and I built out this crisis simulation, which was scheduled to unfold over four hours that morning, we were certain that they would have it managed easily within two hours.

Colt, our good colleague and friend Garth Rowan, and I stood—coffees in hand—ready and waiting in the reception area of our client's highrise. And then we see her. The woman sent to retrieve us has a look of foreboding. Turns out, five people called in sick that morning (we had a hunch that it may have had something to do with the morning exercise that was about to take place), and the team was scrambling to replace them for the exercise.

With the first challenge of the day resolved, the organization's executive team began to file into the boardroom. We briefed them on the goals of the exercise and how it would unfold, and then sent them back to their offices to work until they were summoned—if they were to be summoned at all.

To give you some context, the briefing went something like this:

Good morning!

The goal of today is to test your crisis ready program and to hone the team's crisis management skills. Over the past several months we have worked closely with (let's call her) Sally to develop a crisis scenario that feels extremely real. Your task this morning will be to work together to manage this crisis to the best of your ability. The simulation will unfold over the course of the next four hours and will either escalate or de-escalate according to the team's management of the scenario.

The exercise will begin once your social media team logs into our system. This system is secure and controlled, and simulates the digital landscape including social media, Google search, media sites, blogs, and more.

Once your social media team logs in, they will discover something fishy. It will be up to them to quickly assess the situation and determine whether or not it needs to be escalated—and how to go about that escalation. If and when they decide to escalate, it will be up to each of you to follow the organization's procedures and decide on the right courses of action in order to quickly manage the many dynamics of this crisis that will unfold.

Colt will be in a back room running the digital side of things while role-players may call in, acting as your key stakeholders and expecting answers to their questions and concerns. Meanwhile, Garth and I will act as flies on the wall, observing the events of the day. At the end of the four hours, we will debrief together over lunch.

Now remember: this is only a test of your program, not a test of yourselves or your team. This is the time to make mistakes, learn, and grow together. There are no right or wrong answers, just a group experience. I always say that we all hope to never experience a crisis, but if one were to strike, we would all hope to have experience. This is your time to gain that experience. So, with that said, enjoy, breathe, and have fun!"

Does this sound intriguing (and maybe a little nerve-wracking) to you? Does it sound like an exercise that would help you test and strengthen your program and begin to implement a crisis ready culture? I hope so, because it definitely is!

The fact is, no matter how much thought and time you put into developing your crisis ready program, there will always be kinks and gaps that are only discoverable when the program is put to the test. You certainly don't want to wait for a crisis to strike to test the program and discover these mendable kinks.

Conducting this type of crisis simulation is the next step in the development of your program and the cementing of your culture. Benjamin Franklin once said:

 Tell me and I forget. Teach me and I remember. Involve me and I learn."

Crisis simulations are full-on involving!

In the following pages, we are going to explore the dynamics of this type of exercise and I'm going to walk you through the development of a crisis simulation scenario that will help you achieve some specific goals.

Are you excited? Let's get started!

NOT A TABLETOP EXERCISE

You may be familiar with the tabletop exercise. The tabletop is the original (and, in my opinion, a boring and less-than-practical) way to put an organization's crisis ready program and skills to the test. Now, don't get me wrong; if the goal is to provoke thoughtful discussion, a strong tabletop exercise will help you do that. But so will a simulation, and there's so much more that you can achieve in the same amount of time by taking the simulation approach. Before we begin to develop your simulation, let's be clear on what the difference is between a tabletop exercise and crisis simulation.

Simply put, a tabletop is a theoretical exercise, while a simulation is a practical one. For example, during a tabletop exercise, the organizer will introduce some well-thought-out, high-risk scenarios to the table and ask the crisis management team what they would do. This will inspire dialogue and get people thinking and planning. After the scenario has been discussed for a while, the organizer will verbally introduce another element. Maybe this is a new development, or maybe it entails a jump forward to the second day of the simulated crisis. During the conversations, the team will be required to think through the actions they would take in these situations and raise any questions or concerns they may have.

A simulation, on the other hand, takes a more realistic approach. For example, instead of having someone dictate a summary of the situation to the team, you will field calls from role-players, be presented with news articles, have to navigate social media, and more. The biggest difference is that instead of having the team *discuss* what they would do, they actually have to *get up and do it*.

In a tabletop exercise, you may say something like, "and then we'd have the communications department draft a letter to customers, explaining X, Y, and Z." In a simulation, the right person actually has to get up and communicate this task to the communications department, have them draft the message, get it approved, and send it out to "customers" using a simulation of your dissemination process, gaining their real-time input and feedback.

See the difference? Doesn't a simulation sound so much more fun and impactful as a team-building exercise, when compared to a tabletop? Because simulations are conducted live—in a controlled, secure, and safe environment—as the team manages the simulated incident, the organizer can either turn up the heat or simulate the resolution of the crisis, depending on the team's actions and communications. This means that the exercise provides instantaneous feedback that you have to adapt and respond to, just as you would in a real crisis.

Learn more about the value of a crisis simulation: melissaagnes.com/ simulation

I once conducted a crisis simulation where my client's communications team was taking far too long to respond to the incident. They had aligned on their course of action and the leadership team had approved the next steps, but I watched as their wordsmithing lost them valuable time. So, my team and I decided to turn up the heat.

To do this, we released a video on behalf of a simulated activist group onto our simulated YouTube page. The video insinuated that, due to the company's lack of concern on the cause and effect of the incident, this activist group was going to pay a little visit to the CEO's house. It was a mob mentality sort of thing, and our simulated social media ate it up.

When the client's social media team caught wind of this development, they immediately reported it to the executive and communication teams. They also brilliantly thought to call the company's security team to ensure the safety of the CEO and her family—alerting them to the fact that this was a drill, of course—which was impressive to watch. Through the execution of this escalation inject, the team learned a valuable lesson on time wasted on *words*, when it was the *message* and the act of communicating that their stakeholders were waiting for and cared about.

This is the value of a simulation. The team learns important lessons and gains instant feedback. However, as you can probably imagine, a rewarding simulation requires a lot of elaborate thought and planning. For example, we anticipated the need for the activist video in the development stages of the exercise, but only activated it if the moment called for it. So how do you anticipate the different directions that the team may take throughout the exercise? The answer comes down to three things: creativity, thorough planning, and in-the-moment flexibility. Let's break this down and get you developing an effective—and fun—crisis simulation!

MAKING IT COUNT

First, identify the goals and objectives of the exercise. What is it that you want to achieve? The answer will depend on your organization, its current crisis preparedness, and any pre-identified (or anticipated) gaps that you'd like to focus on. For example, some goals and objectives I've worked to meet with different clients include things like:

- Identifying areas within the crisis ready program and governance structure that may need to be strengthened.

- Testing the organization's corporate communications function in relation to crisis management, including internal and external communication practices and processes.

- Helping the team better understand today's crisis management realities and stakeholder expectations.

- Testing the team's ability to manage all aspects of a real-world, real-time crisis, including social media and the never-ending news cycle.

- Helping to strengthen the team's crisis management skills, confidence, and experience in situations where the stakes are high and the pressure is intense.

- Focusing on team-building and strengthening cross-department relationships.

Identifying your goals and objectives will give you focus and clarity when developing the details of the exercise. Take a moment to reflect on what it is you would like to achieve, test, or strengthen through this process and jot it down. Remember that you don't need to achieve everything at once. You can always—and in fact, you should—conduct other exercises in the future. So, start with your primary objectives.

DEVELOPING THE SCENARIO

Great! You have established the goals and objectives that will guide the development of the exercise. The next step is to determine the best crisis scenario to simulate. This is often the most challenging part! You want to choose a high-risk scenario that aligns with your stated objectives while also having enough flexibility to be elaborate and multi-dimensional, or contained, depending on who is taking part in the exercise.

If your entire crisis management team is taking part, you can go full-throttle with your scenario and make it as complex and dynamic as you want. On the other hand, if your exercise is restricted to a specific segment of your team, then you'll need to work towards developing a scenario that meets the objectives and is dynamic enough to test the team's full capabilities, but does not impact areas of the business that are not part of the exercise.

To help you choose the type of crisis you will simulate, refer to your list of high-risk scenarios and begin talking through what a scenario might look like, and whether it will help you meet your stated objectives.

It's also important to note that the element of surprise is critical for a successful simulation. This means that, while people may know that the exercise will take place, they don't know much more than that. So, when developing the scenario, be sure to work with outside experts or internal colleagues that will not play a role in managing the exercise. If you happen to be a part of the crisis management team, then you probably shouldn't be a part of the developmental process of the exercise either! If you are a part of it, however, then make sure you don't take part in the actual exercise. Instead, this is a great opportunity to have your designated alternate test out their crisis management abilities.

Once you have the high-risk scenario chosen, it is time to get specific. Don't be afraid to be creative, and be ready to play a whole lot of devil's advocate to test out ideas and see how well they may work. For example, if you chose a cybersecurity incident as your high-risk scenario, start determining the specifics of the situation. This will require thought and discussions with the appropriate people. Here is an example of what that thought process might look like:

How did the incident occur?

Was it a maliciously planned attack, a computer malfunction, or an employee error that left the organization exposed? Refer back to your three categories of events from chapter seven to help you answer this question.

What is the extent of the impact?

What will be breached? The organization's data? Its systems? Perhaps both? And what is the impact of the breach? Work with your IT department to gather the details.

How much will you confirm at the beginning of the exercise?

How will you provide this confirmed information to the team? Will the conductor explain it in words? Will IT call the crisis management team with the details? Or might the team read about it on social media? If so, how did it get there?

At what point will news of the incident become public?

Will the media be reporting at the start of the exercise, or will the team have some time before news gets out? How and when will the news get out? Will an employee leak it, or will the hackers brag about their actions? Or perhaps the data will be found online somewhere? If so, will it be evident that it was your organization that was breached, or will there be insinuations and hunches, but no direct confirmation?

How will the exercise continue to unfold?

Will IT keep calling in with updates? What will those updates be? What twists and turns might you be able to fit into these updates?

How will the exercise escalate?

What sorts of injects can you design for these escalations? Will stakeholders begin to call in with questions and concerns? Will rumors and speculation begin to form on social media, making their way into the news media? Will activist groups begin to target the organization, leveraging this crisis to help them further their own agendas?

Who needs to be involved in its development?

Whom do you need to work with to make sure that all injects, escalations, and new developments are realistic and made the most of?

What if the team manages the simulation exceptionally well?

How can you either turn up or down the heat in a realistic way? Also, how can you demonstrate their exceptional crisis management in a natural way? Will fans and customers begin to show their support on social media? Will news media begin to report on the organization's excellent crisis communication?

How will the exercise end?

Will you just declare it "over" at a certain time, or will you incorporate a fun element? One of my favorites for a cybersecurity scenario is, "the FBI has instructed us to cease all activity. They are about to overtake the forensics investigation and have forbidden us to communicate with stakeholders for at least several days."

There are many elements to a crisis and the more thorough the development of the scenario, the better the exercise will be. The reality is that you can never fully anticipate how the team will react and manage the incident, so you want to prepare for anything. This means that you will probably develop more content than you will use during the exercise, but that's okay. For example, when we developed the inject of the activist video I mentioned earlier, I remember thinking it was overkill. Then, when it became evident that it would be a great spontaneous twist, I was so grateful to Garth for having thought of it. It was the perfect inject to demonstrate an important point. So be creative and thorough, and have fun!

PUTTING THE PIECES TOGETHER

Once you have determined the details, it's time to bring the exercise to life. I usually start by thoroughly mapping out the entirety of the exercise in order to stay focused and organized. Depending on the details of the scenario and the injects you have created, you may choose to incorporate the following pieces to your exercise:

Scripts

Which stakeholders will call in, at what point, and whom will they call? Who will play these roles? What will they ask? What will they demand? Will they be angry, confused, annoyed, worried, scared, etc.?

Ask employees who are not a part of the exercise to take on these roles. Find people who are enthusiastic about this opportunity, as enthusiasm makes for great role-players. I mean, when else will they get the opportunity to put their managers or bosses under direct heat?!

Be sure to brief them thoroughly, let them know to keep this hush-hush, and to provide them with a script and the correct numbers to call. It's also a good idea to have a two-way line of communication set up with them so you can give them a ping when it's time to make a call or take on a new role.

Additionally, ask them to document the experience. For example, how long did it take to get a callback? Was the team member resistant? Did they say too much? Were they too emotional? This feedback will come in handy during the debriefing at the end of the exercise, and can provide in-the-moment inspiration for additional injects!

News articles and blog posts

Release these at the appropriate times, throughout the exercise. I usually use these as a way to provide additional tidbits of information to the team, as well as to intensify some real-world challenges.

Start by deciding on the appropriate media outlets and bloggers to simulate. Who would realistically report on this type of scenario, including industry-related outlets and scenario-related outlets? Then, before drafting the articles, do some research to determine tone of voice, specific angles, questions, and other details that would be part of these articles and posts.

From there, map out when these articles will be "published" throughout the course of the exercise.

Social media

If you are incorporating social media into your exercise, then choose the channels and platforms that make sense for your organization, its stakeholders, and your crisis preparedness. You should have a solid understanding of this information, since you have already worked through chapters three and seven.

It is important that you *not* use your real channels! The last thing you want is to confuse your real stakeholders, or worse, launch your organization into a real crisis! This is where the technology aspect can really be an advantage, which I'll get to in a moment.

The point of bringing social media into the exercise it to intensify the challenges for your team. When developing the pieces of a client's simulation, I draft several hundred social media posts in preparation for the exercise. Sometimes I will incorporate images and video, if it will help reinforce lessons and make the exercise more realistic and impactful.

Determine how often you will post to each simulated platform. For example, how often will you tweet? Perhaps there will be scarce chatter on social media at the start of the exercise, which will gradually increase as the scenario escalates. To determine this, think through the typical amount of mentions your organization gets on a given day, the timeline of your exercise, the injections, points of escalation, points of de-escalation, and news articles. Use social media to help bring these elements to life.

While I always create my content in advance, I also make sure to incorporate some real-time social media posts. So, account for flexibility. Odds are the team will give you a lot of inspiration as they work through managing the scenario—which is part of *your* fun, as the conductor of the exercise!

THE USE OF TECHNOLOGY

Personally, I like to use technology when conducting simulations for clients. It adds a real-world element that goes a long way towards keeping people engaged. There are companies out there that offer this type of service through the use of secure web-based platforms that simulate everything, including social media, Google search results pages, news media, blogs, and more.

This type of technology offers realism and two-way engagement to your exercise. For example, when your team releases an update to your simulated website and pushes it out through the simulated social media channels, the conductor of the exercise will get to engage with them directly. They can use social media and the news sites to spin your words, ask questions, share concerns, make demands, and retweet your messages, as appropriate.

However, even though this technology offers incredible advantages, it's not the technology itself that is important. It's the *simulation of real-world impact*. There are a multitude of other ways you can recreate these aspects internally if you don't have the budget or resources to work with a company that can provide this type of service. For example, instead of demonstrating the latest news articles on a fancy web-based platform, you can simply print them and circulate them to the appropriate people at the appropriate times.

The elements, and how they're incorporated with an eye to making the simulation as real and engaging as possible, are the most valuable aspects of this process. In my experience, people don't mind using their imaginations. If you do your job right when it comes to developing an engaging and realistic scenario, they'll fall right into their roles and you'll achieve the results you're looking to achieve.

THE DEBRIEFING STAGE

My personal preference is to conduct the simulation in the morning, as everyone is at their freshest, and then to debrief over lunch. The objectives of this debrief are to:

- Allow the team to process their experience.

- Share opinions and reflect on the experience, the scenario, and the effects of the exercise.

- Identify and discuss the group's strengths.

- Identify and discuss any gaps or weaknesses that may have been revealed.

- Discuss and align on next steps for strengthening the program and continuing to strengthen the organization's crisis ready culture.

As the conductor of the simulation, it's important to take notes throughout the exercise and share these observations during the debriefing stage. However, it is also important to let the team reflect and discuss their own observations, and give them the opportunity to process the results that transpired. This debriefing stage should take no longer than an hour and should conclude with everyone agreeing on some actionable takeaways that will help the team continue to evolve its crisis readiness.

BETTER IS ALWAYS POSSIBLE

Even the most crisis ready organizations gain tons of value from this type of exercise, because crisis preparedness is an evolutionary process. There is always something to learn and strengthen. For example, the client I mentioned at the start of this chapter performs these types of exercises on a yearly basis. Even with that amount of training, they always leave the exercise with lessons learned and steps to implement. To give you an idea, the day that we performed the exercise I shared with you, they learned the following:

**People were too hung up on fine-tuning words, which
resulted in less timely communication.**

This is a common phenomenon—one that is negatively impactful and,
therefore, important to overcome. The way we helped the team realize this
hiccup on their own was to continue to intensify the challenges the longer
they took to respond.

The way I see it, my goal as a consultant is to help my clients realize these
types of things on their own as much as possible, and then to be there to help
them better understand the potential impact and identify strategic solutions.
The more I can help my clients come to their own realizations, or draw their
own conclusions, the more likely (and enthusiastic) they will be to strengthen
or overcome their weaknesses.

**There was an unnecessary disconnect between the media
relations and social media teams.**

Both groups were being asked similar questions, and yet because they were not
communicating with one another, they were forced to needlessly do twice the
work in drafting responses. They also could have given each other a heads-up
regarding the types of questions and concerns they were being asked, which
would have resulted in more streamlined and efficient external communication.

During the debriefing stage, we determined that these two groups needed
to a) communicate more with one another and b) physically be closer to each
other. We implemented this adjustment in the appropriate areas of the crisis
ready program.

**People's characteristic traits resulted in a broken
telephone effect.**

While this was no one's fault, it was a problem that needed to be resolved.
For example, the social media team was tasked with providing hourly updates
to the executive team. The person responsible for these updates is a very
quiet, introverted person by nature. This personality trait resulted in him not

effectively communicating the urgency of some of the incidents taking place on social media, which meant that the executive team felt they had more time to develop a solution or strategy of response than they truly did.

The solution, which we determined during the debriefing stage of the exercise, was to equip the war room with a monitor so that the executive team could always have access to social media and keep their fingers on this pulse if they needed to.

The crisis war room was physically too small.

With the number of people who were walking in and out of the room throughout the exercise, the team realized that the room was too small and that this was hampering crisis management efforts. For example, they chose to call members of the team for updates rather than asking them to come into the room for in-person discussions, since there wasn't enough room! Had those members been physically present, things may have gone differently and more smoothly.

The takeaway here was to choose a bigger boardroom to designate as the organization's crisis war room.

These particular lessons are extremely important, and identifying them allowed the team to strengthen weaknesses. You will have noticed that they are things that can *only* be identified by experiencing a crisis...or, better yet, by experiencing a crisis simulation!

FURTHER CONSIDERATIONS

I have been asked many questions over the years about crisis simulations. These come from prospective and current clients, friends, and people who are just plain curious. I've selected a few of them to answer in order to give you a complete picture of the nuances to this approach.

How often should you perform this type of exercise?

This depends on your organization. Some organizations have complete control over when and where they conduct simulations, while other organizations are under tight industry regulations that require drills on a yearly basis. If your industry does not have such requirements, then I recommend conducting this type of drill every twelve, eighteen, or twenty-four months at the maximum.

Each time you conduct a simulation, you can choose to target different goals, as well as practice the tactics learned from the previous exercise. The scenario will also change, which always makes the exercise a new and fun challenge and experience for everyone involved.

How long does it generally take to develop a crisis simulation?

It will probably take anywhere between three and five months to develop a full-scale simulation, especially if it isn't your full-time job. Between determining the right scenario, gathering the necessary information to make the exercise realistic, developing the injects and escalations, and putting the pieces together, there is a lot of work that goes into these exercises. The good news is that it's entirely worth the effort!

Do people respond differently to a crisis simulation, versus a real crisis, as they know it's a drill?

Not if you do a thorough job at developing a realistic exercise. When you conduct a simulation, people tend to show up knowing that they need to give it their all. The more realistic you make the scenario and its injects, the more engagement you'll get and the more real the scenario will feel.

Should you take your team by surprise?

In other words, should you not tell them you are planning on conducting a simulation? This depends on you and your team. Will this element of surprise add value to the exercise? It may and it may not. This is up to you to decide—just make sure you get approval first!

Should you tell your external stakeholders about these exercises?

It depends on the stakeholder and the purpose of sharing this information. For example, sharing this with your board of directors or investors may inspire additional confidence in the organization and its crisis preparedness and prevention. However, sharing it with your clients may be unnecessary.

When determining with whom and how you share this information, identify the goal and potential impact of doing so. Will it add value and help you build trust and credibility, or might it spark concern, or simply be a needless share?

How easy should it be to beat the scenario?

Not easy! You want to challenge your team and the program. The scenario should be realistic and complex. If the team does successfully manage the simulated crisis, while that's great news, it will also be an indicator to up the ante for the next exercise. However, even if this proves to be the case, there will still be valuable lessons to take away. There always are!

You can't validate your program until you have tested it. A crisis simulation gives your team the opportunity to test each element of the program, while experiencing the pressures of a crisis firsthand. Your team will have the chance to make mistakes and learn from them, gaining experience that they would not otherwise have gained and cultivating skills that will make them better, more efficient communicators and decision makers in times of crisis.

With that said, good luck and have fun—and do let me know how it goes! I'd love to hear about your crisis simulation experience, the lessons and takeaways you learned, and how it helped the organization implement its crisis ready culture.

And with this, I want to congratulate you! You have completed the homework pages of this book and now have everything you need to develop a strong and scalable crisis ready program, as well as implement a rewarding crisis ready culture. Well done!

While you still have one last chapter to read, it will be a fun one—you have certainly earned some fun! In chapter ten, we are going to dissect some interesting case studies. We'll do a comparative analysis, and look at some great crisis management initiatives (and a few terrible ones) up against your newly developed crisis ready program and culture. I'm also going to discuss some remaining important and challenging topics through the examination of some interesting real-world case studies.

Are you ready for the final stretch? Let's do it!

10

CONTROVERSIES, TROLLS, EBOLA, AND YOU

We've discussed a lot over the course of this book, but there are still a few points that need addressing. In fact, I would be left feeling as though this book was incomplete if I didn't discuss them. Why? Mainly because they're important, and often difficult to face. And I want you to be armed and ready. They're also common topics of interest when I'm on stage, presenting my seminars and programs to audiences just like you. So why not take the opportunity?

However, you've done a lot of work over the course of the last nine chapters, and you deserve to unwind and have some fun, so I thought I would discuss these remaining topics through the exploration of some interesting case studies.

As we discuss each incident and its management, I recommend trying to put yourself in the shoes of the organizations and thinking through what your management approach might be, and how you would implement the crisis ready tactics and strategies you've learned throughout this book.

With all that said, let's jump into the first story!

CONTROVERSIES ARE TRICKY

Imagine a scenario where a member of your management team unwittingly goes on the record with a comment that results in segregating your target audience. While this comment was unscripted and ad hoc, meaning it was said on an emotional whim and the consequences were not thought through or anticipated, it ended up being impactful.

This was a situation that Marcus Lemonis, the TV reality star and chairman and CEO of Camping World, found himself in in the summer of 2017. A few days following the white nationalists rally in Charlottesville, VA, in August 2017, Lemonis made the following statement in an interview with CNBC:[31]

> There's no doubt that there is probably not many consumers in this country today that are in favor of what has been said in the last couple days and if they are, quite frankly, don't shop at my business."

This was Lemonis's response to some of the statements made by President Donald J. Trump immediately following the rally, when he discussed that there was "blame on both sides" of the rally and protest.

Let me be clear. I'm not getting political here. My intent is only to discuss a situation that stemmed from an unscripted, emotional statement, and the impact it threatened to have on the brand. Why? Because Lemonis is not the first, nor will he be the last, to find himself in such a predicament. What if the next time something like this happens, it is your organization that is dragged into controversy?

> CRISIS READY Rule: Emotion always overpowers reason.

It is important to remember that your organization is made up of human beings. Sometimes emotion can overcome even the best of us. Lemonis made the statement he made on a whim. He was speaking from a place of personal conviction. And on this whim, this abrupt statement segregated his audience.

I am sure you can imagine what happened next. The media took off with the story and Lemonis was criticized, with many taking to social media to threaten his physical safety. Others talked about boycotting Camping World. The fact that Camping World caters to customers of all different political positions meant that this statement, and the upset it caused, risked having a negative impact on the organization's business.

What would
you do?

Before you say that this situation would never happen to your organization, the reality is that it can. Your organization is made up of human beings, not robots!

> **CRISIS READY Rule: The more you think you don't need a crisis ready program, the more desperately you DO need one.**

Therefore, before I proceed with what happened next, I want you to take a moment and reflect.

- If you were to find yourself in a similar situation, would you categorize this incident as an issue or a crisis? Why, and under what circumstances might that classification change?

- What would be your strategy of response?

_____

_____

_____

_____

_____

_____

_____

THE BEST STRATEGY OF RESPONSE

Because of Camping World's demographics and Lemonis's celebrity status, this issue went viral quickly and had the potential to escalate to crisis level. Therefore, this issue needed to be addressed. How do you come back from such a bold, controversial statement that has managed to incite such a strong, emotional response? The key is to be thoughtful, decisive, and clear. Then, leave the situation be. Let people vent, and let the incident die out on its own while you continue to monitor.

Be thoughtful

In this particular scenario, the initial statement was made hastily. This means that the organization was forced to reflect and decide whether the statement aligned with the company's values or not. Does Lemonis stand by his statement and hold strong, or does he, upon further reflection, conclude that the statement was hasty and does not truly reflect the sentiment or values of Camping World?

Be decisive

Once the decision has been made, a stance needs to be taken. Because we're talking about a deeply controversial and emotional topic, being decisive is essential. It would cause more damage to take a stance and then turn around and make a retraction. There will be risk, no matter what the decision is, as some people are bound to be upset. This risk should be understood and accepted prior to taking an official stance.

Be clear

When you come out with your response to the situation, you need to be clear. Don't ambiguously leave room for misinterpretation or misconception. You want to address the issue as needed and put it to bed.

WHAT LEMONIS DID...AND SHOULD HAVE DONE

Upon reflection, Lemonis decided that his initial statement had been rushed and emotional, and that it therefore lacked clarity. He felt that, as a result, it had been taken out of context. To address this, he came out with a series of statements.

His first official response took the form of a livestream video,[32] where he attempted to clarify his statement by saying, "if you are okay with what was said in Charlottesville, and what was done, that I'm not okay with it." He went on to talk about how, no matter what your stance is, we have to permit freedom of speech, and that he draws the line at violence and hatred.

While the message of this video clearly was that he is against violence and hatred, it did nothing to address the "don't shop at my business" statement, the one that caused the upset in the first place. His video was more of an emotional ramble, not the thoughtful, decisive, and clear message he needed to make. As a result, it did not succeed in putting the issue to bed.

A couple days later, he followed this video up with another explanation, this time as a Facebook post. This open letter was another long ramble. He talked about being bullied as a child, being sensitive as an adult, and being a human that has made tons of mistakes. When he finally got to the point, he shared some good messages. For example, he wrote:

- "The mistake I made in the last week was not being clear."

- "While I stand strong on my position that violence, hate, bigotry is unacceptable from anyone regardless of what side you are on and that all of us need to be accountable, only I am accountable for my actions."

- "Last week I gave my opinion on what had happened. I made the mistake of letting my fear and emotion talk about subjects that I shouldn't have."

- "As the CEO of a business, I am responsible to take care of the people that work there. I opened my mouth and put them in harms way. While I know, that the headline published was taken out of context and I have to live with that, there should have never been a headline and I gave [it] a chance to live."

- "My apology is sincere. It is to my employees who have been forced to deal with this. I am nothing without you. I am here to serve, guide and protect you. I will work harder. Please forgive me. Please don't punish them."

- "I apologize to anyone who has supported their cause, their political preference, their candidate, their beliefs. I was not raised this way and have always been taught to respect everyone. This is a free county and my fears shouldn't be projected on anyone. I am asking for your forgiveness. I should have not disrespected that and will not again."

- "I apologize to the people who have followed my show for years and have said they have learned so much and are inspired, who now say that have been let down and will never trust me again."

There are some good messages hidden in here. However, due to the rambling, the lack of clarity, and decisiveness, the entirety of his response was difficult to read. It was, once again, too emotional. It also contained, as he put it, "typos and grammar mistakes all over this free form written document."

There is no reason why any type of apology or official response statement, issued on behalf of an organization or a personal brand, should be a "free form document"! It needs to be thoughtful, succinct, and strong. It needs to obviously state your main message points in a compassionate and relatable manner. The only reason why Lemonis needed to make two statements was that he did not come out with one strong one to begin with. He should have. It would have been in his favor to do so.

Imagine if, instead of two rambling statements, he came out with one strong statement that said something like:

> Last week, in my interview with CNBC, I mistakenly spoke out of fear and emotion and, as a result, I did not properly communicate the message I intended to. Let me now be clear. I do not condone hatred, discrimination, or violence in any form, or at any time. I do, however, strongly believe that we are all entitled to our own beliefs and I apologize for, myself, having discriminated against those whose beliefs are different from mine. Our freedom to choose and believe as we wish is part of what makes this country great. That said, I strongly believe that this freedom should be expressed without infringing upon the same rights and freedom of others, and without violence or hatred.
>
> I also want to apologize to the hard-working individuals that work at our many locations. Through my mistake, I put you in harm's way and I am truly sorry. You did not deserve that. It is my job to protect and guide you, and I won't make such a mistake again. Thank you for all that you do."

When this situation happened, it was an issue that needed to be monitored and only addressed upon escalation. This means that Lemonis had the luxury of a little more time, in relation to some of the timelines we've discussed throughout this book. As he had the luxury of time, he should have used it to think, decide on his stance, and draft a solid response that would have helped him quickly end the whole fiasco.

WHEN CAGED BY TROLLS

Do you remember the Emory University Hospital case study we discussed in chapter two? At the time when this story was unfolding back in 2014 some people proposed closing down Emory's social media channels, as the viral backlash was detracting from their important messages and work. This was a bad idea that, thankfully, Emory never even considered. Instead, they used the social media retaliation to better understand the emotions that were fueling the situation's escalation, and were then able to overcome the negative, and take control of the narrative of the incident.

My point in bringing this story back up is to highlight the fact that, typically, when people consider going dark on social media, they do so out of a misguided fear or an inability to manage a negative viral situation. But as we've seen throughout this book, this fear is misplaced.

CRISIS READY Rule: Social media is the gasoline, not the fire. (It can also be the smoke and the rainbow.)

So, I want to take this opportunity to address a commonly posed question:

When is it okay to close your social media accounts as a response to a crisis or an issue? Is it ever okay to do this?

Before I answer, I want you to really think about this. Under what types of circumstances would you feel it worthwhile to discuss this action as an option with your team? Take a minute to reflect before turning the page.

Do you remember the devastating incident that happened in May of 2016, when a three-year-old boy fell into Harambe the gorilla's enclosure at the Cincinnati Zoo and Botanical Garden? The zoo's Dangerous Animal Response Team took swift action, making the decision to fatally shoot the gorilla to save the young boy's life.

The incident was, of course, caught on video and quickly went viral.

> **CRISIS READY Rule: Always assume there's video.**

The zoo did everything right in managing this unfortunate crisis. They quickly and decisively took action to save the child's life; they communicated compassionately, in a timely fashion, and with complete transparency;[33] they took measures to reinforce the security of their gorilla barriers, post-incident; and they honored Harambe's memory in multiple ways. While their community grieved with and supported the zoo, others did not.

Over the course of the months following this tragic event, the Cincinnati Zoo suffered continuous and relentless online harassment and spam. Hundreds of petitions were published, accumulating thousands upon thousands of signatures. These petitions ranged between everything from "Justice for Harambe" to "Make Harambe a Pokémon" to making "Harambe Day a Cincinnati Zoo Tradition." Hashtags such as #JusticeForHarambe, #RIPHarambe, and even #DicksOutForHarambe were used across all sorts of social media platforms, in many ridiculous and irrelevant ways. Memes continued to be created and shared and Thane Maynard, the Cincinnati Zoo director, had his Twitter account hacked. The spam and harassment was relentless. Anytime the zoo posted a message to its Facebook or Twitter accounts, it was met with an abundance of spam and abusive comments.

Through these months of virtual abuse and viral spam, the zoo continued with their business and regular social media activity, while they mourned the loss of their beloved gorilla. Finally, when it would not cease, in August of 2016

Maynard pleaded with people to stop the insensitivity and harassing behavior by issuing the following statement via the *Associated Press*:[34]

> We are not amused by the memes, petitions and signs about Harambe. Our zoo family is still healing, and the constant mention of Harambe makes moving forward more difficult for us. We are honoring Harambe by redoubling our gorilla conservation efforts and encouraging others to join us."

Unfortunately, Maynard's plea didn't work, and his Twitter account was hacked again. The zoo also received a threat from the hacker himself, telling them that their official Twitter account would be next.

WHAT WOULD YOU DO?

What would you do if you were faced with this type of relentless targeting? How long would you put up with it? It seems like an impossible situation, doesn't it? No matter what you do, you're met with an abundance of spam. However, at the same time, business continues to operate well and your key stakeholders and community continue to support you.

WHAT DID THE ZOO DO?

In August of 2016, after their Twitter account was threatened, the Cincinnati Zoo decided to shut it down for the time being. This decision was clearly not made lightly. It wasn't a knee-jerk reaction to the virality of the incident, nor to the backlash. It was a contemplative action to protect their account and key stakeholders from further abuse after months of being subjected to abusive online behavior that, as Maynard put it, was preventing the zoo family from moving forward and healing.

It is a rare event when closing your social media channels is the right course of action. In this case, the zoo had exhausted all other options and needed to move forward, past the ubiquitous spam. While their other social media channels enabled them to put up various filters to block much of the abusive behavior, Twitter did not offer these same capabilities—not to mention that their Twitter account was also in jeopardy. The zoo made the right call by shutting it down.

While many of the internet trolls were ready and waiting for them when they reactivated their Twitter account in October of that same year—after putting in additional security measures to help mitigate the risk of a targeted hack—the majority of them had moved on. At the time of this writing, the zoo shared with me that not a day goes by that they don't encounter some kind of message about or image of Harambe, but they have put their focus on moving forward. Since then, they have welcomed Fiona, the baby hippo, into the world!

I know what some of you might be thinking. Was this a social media crisis? And I see your point. But let me ask you this: was this a crisis?

Remember the definition of a crisis, which we discussed back in chapter four? A crisis is a negative event or situation that impacts, or threatens to impact, people, the environment, business operations, the organization's reputation, and / or the organization's bottom line over the long-term. So, knowing what you know about this situation, was this a crisis?

The answer is no, it was not. The crisis happened when the child's life was in danger. The internet troll aspect of the situation did not cause, nor did it threaten to cause, negative material long-term impact to the Cincinnati Zoo. Even though these memes and behaviors were constant, the zoo's operations continued, and their stakeholders, i.e., their community, their employees, and their customers, continued to support them. Therefore, the online aspect of this situation was a viral issue that needed to be managed appropriately. They managed it by getting great at using filters, and by temporarily deactivating their Twitter account. When they reinstated their account, they made sure to design protocols that would help them use Twitter in a way that would reduce the risk of provoking more of this behavior.

CRISIS READY Rule: There is no such thing as a social media crisis!

A NEW WORLD CALLS FOR NEW STRATEGIES

Before we close out this book, I want to leave you with one last story. I've saved this story specifically for the end of this book simply because it's one of my all-time favorites. It's one of those stories that continues to inspire me, year after year, each new time I share it with my audiences from the stage. It's the story of how the world-crisis of Ebola was effectively managed.

In 2014, the Ebola virus was ferociously spreading throughout the West African countries of Guinea, Liberia, and Sierra Leone, taking thousands of lives. Its march showed little to no signs of stopping. The disease was also starting to spread to other parts of the world, with isolated cases being reported in Italy, Senegal, Spain, the UK, and the United States.

In the summer of 2014, airlines started canceling flights to Guinea, Liberia, and Sierra Leone; in the autumn of 2014, the U.S. imposed specific travel restrictions for people traveling from these countries. This was a rising global crisis that had people around the world growing increasingly concerned.

Dozens of humanitarian organizations, government entities, and NGOs were working tirelessly to manage this escalating epidemic. And yet, it was one unlikely entity that developed the crisis management strategy that began to resolve this rising crisis. Do you know what that entity was?

It was the BBC.

In the summer of 2014, the BBC amped up their coverage of the Ebola crisis and began focusing some of their communications on messages concerning public health, especially in these areas of the world. You see, the BBC knew that one of the biggest reasons why Ebola was spreading so profusely throughout these West African countries was that West Africans don't have the same easy access to education and information that we so readily do—and tend to take for granted—in the first world. As a direct result, they continually and unwittingly exposed themselves to the virus, over and over.

For example, within some cultures, when a loved one passes away, they have a beautiful ritual that brings them in touching contact with their deceased loved one to say goodbye. But no one told them that you can catch Ebola from a dead body! So, with a mission of helping to provide educational information to these areas of the world, the BBC sought to answer the following question:

If education is the answer, how can we seek to directly reach and educate West Africans so as to provide them with the tools, knowledge, and resources to better protect themselves and their loved ones from contracting this terrible disease?

This was the question that many organizations were proactively trying to answer. The difference between the BBC and these countless other organizations was that the BBC had a different mindset and culture. For example, these other organizations were attempting to use more traditional tactics, such as radio and the distribution of pamphlets. These were tactics that have proven to work in the past, but weren't resulting in the required level of reach and education that was needed now.

The BBC took a different approach. They sought to truly understand the stakeholder—the target audience: West Africans. Through their research and past experience, they knew that West Africans, as a society, love the mobile app WhatsApp. It turns out that they use this free text messaging app every day to communicate with family and friends. The team at the BBC saw this as an opportunity to proactively reach this stakeholder on their turf.

So they began to design a strategy that would enable them to do so. They named this strategy the "WhatsApp Ebola Service," and it was relatively simple. They would create a WhatsApp account and work with the app to make sure that their account wouldn't confront any hiccups, such as being blacklisted.

CRISIS READY Rule: Never launch a new product, campaign, or communication without assessing the potential risk.

However,

it was also important that these communications be easily digestible, interesting, and even fun!

They would then market this WhatsApp Ebola Service to their target audience, who could then freely subscribe to the service in the same way they used the app to connect with loved ones. Every day, the BBC would push out three targeted messages, in both English and

Interested in hearing and seeing samples of the communications that were shared via the WhatsApp Ebola Service? Check them out at: melissaagnes.com/bbc

French—the two languages spoken in this region of the world—concerning Ebola and how to keep from contracting it.

However, it was also important that these communications be easily digestible, interesting, and even fun—in other words, emotionally compelling! They couldn't be lengthy news articles, for example, with the information contained somewhere within. Nobody would read that—not to mention that a large portion of the population in this area of the world is illiterate, so not everybody could read that.

In order to achieve maximum reach and consumption, the three pieces of educational information that the BBC disseminated via this WhatsApp Ebola Service were things like illustrations that contained minimal words, and told a story just by looking at them; the BBC collaborated with popular local artists to create short, catchy songs that told a clear message; they released other forms of short audio clips as well, never longer than sixty seconds; and, yes, there were some text message-based messages, for those who preferred to consume written communications.

It worked.[35]

Within just a couple of weeks, many of those other organizations who had been attempting to achieve the same objective came to the BBC and asked how they could collaborate and help the initiative progress even further. An initiative that was launched as a six-week trial ended up lasting over six months, with dozens of entities and organizations, such as many of BBC's internal networks, as well as external organizations such as UNICEF and the World

Health Organization, collaborating on this strategy to manage the world-crisis of Ebola.

One of the great things about this strategy was that as WhatsApp is a text messaging app, it intuitively supports two-way communication. Therefore, West Africans could easily text back to the BBC

I interviewed Trushar Barot, the BBC editor responsible for this initiative, on the Crisis Intelligence Podcast. Tune in here: melissaagnes.com/bbcpodcast

and their partners with specific questions. As these organizations have instant access to information and education, they were easily able to gain answers to those questions, using them to continue to educate and help.

For example, one of the questions they received is whether Ebola can be contracted from mosquitoes. The answer, shockingly, is yes. Theoretically, Ebola can be transmitted by mosquitoes. This information fueled another round of informative communications that warned people about this fact, and provided them with information and tools to mitigate the risk of mosquito bites.

Whether they consciously realize it or not, the BBC has a crisis ready culture. In their mission to help manage the Ebola crisis, they leveraged their culture and mindset to think outside the box and approach this rising epidemic through a very strategic, forward-thinking lens; they comprehensively understood the variables and impacts of this escalating crisis; they identified the ultimate problem and they sought to truly understand the stakeholder; they used this information to proactively design an action plan and a communication strategy; and they quickly implemented the program, which ultimately led to the management of this global crisis. Now that, ladies and gentlemen, is the power of a crisis ready culture!

This can—and I hope, *will*—be you and your organization. After reading this book and implementing the ideology and practices I've shared throughout, there's no reason why it can't be. In fact, you are already well on your way to being truly crisis ready.

I hope that these last examples have helped to answer some remaining questions and solidify the importance of the work you have done thus far, and should continue doing. I also hope that you're ready and excited for the next steps that lay ahead of you, no matter how intense they might be. And on that note...

CONCLUSION

BUILD AN INVINCIBLE BRAND

It's Sunday morning, and as you sit with your morning coffee, you can't help but smile inwardly. The last few days have been chaotic, but you and your team have successfully pulled through.

After learning about the train derailment, you quickly convened with your fellow *TrainCompany* executives, and initiated an investigation into the event. While you do not yet have all the answers, you have since been working closely with the authorities and the team is determined to get to the bottom of how such an event occurred—and do whatever is needed to prevent a reoccurrence, to the greatest extent possible.

Your social media team, who learned about the incident before you did, had instantly begun monitoring the news media coverage and online activity. By the time you called them in, they had already triaged a list of pertinent questions and concerns that were being expressed. This list helped your communications team quickly draft, finalize, and disseminate a first response statement to your key stakeholders. You have since been committed to proactive, transparent, and compassionate communications.

As your employees rolled into work on Wednesday morning, they had already received an initial communication from the executive team, providing them with information and directives for the day ahead. They all came together and did a tremendous job, implementing their individual roles and responsibilities with aplomb.

TrainCompany is providing ongoing support to those who have been impacted. You've noticed that there's a greater sense of community that has managed to come out of this devastating situation. While service operations are still down, and will be for at least another week in the affected area, your team managed to own the narrative of the crisis. Through your actions, words, and commitments, your key stakeholders know that you are committed to doing what is right, and they trust the information you release in your updates.

This was a major incident, with lots of unfortunate consequences, but you're proud of your team. They were crisis ready and, as a result, the organization will progress forward with deeper, more loyal relationships with its many stakeholders.

Now that you are fully equipped with the tools and knowledge to become crisis ready, it's time to commit to the required actions. Do this, and you will build an invincible brand. A brand that is composed of unbreakable relationships, with a team that will instinctively overcome any challenge in real time with increased organizational credibility, trust and goodwill. This is a powerful phenomenon—a phenomenon that is entirely within your reach, which means you have no excuse to not act!

Your work clearly doesn't end when you close this book; nor does it end with the completion of the development of your crisis ready program. You haven't created a crisis management plan that will sit, collecting dust on a shelf, after all. Rather, you've begun to implement a crisis ready culture that will continue to serve your organization. And culture requires ongoing effort from the top down, and from the bottom up.

CRISIS READY MODEL

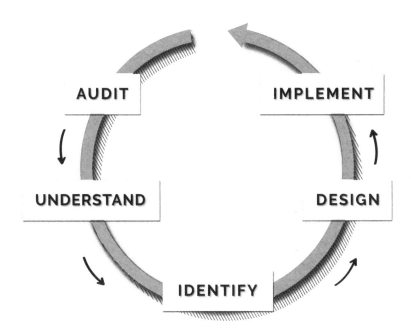

So, before you close this book and continue with your day, I'll ask you to do one final thing. Put thought into the following, and hold yourself and your team accountable for its implementation.

CHOOSE YOUR NEXT STEPS

What action items are remaining from this book, and how will you commit to undertaking them? What does that timeline look like, and what are the ultimate objectives you aim to achieve? How will you continue to embed this culture of readiness, vigilance, and increased stakeholder value within your organization? How will you encourage, empower, and reward the continued efforts of your team? What steps will you proactively take every day to continue to strengthen stakeholder trust, and thus gain the opportunity of having the benefit of the doubt at the onset of an incident?

What you choose to do now, after reading this book, is what will make all the difference. The choice and power is yours, so choose wisely. Choose to gain from all the benefits that a crisis ready culture will offer. Choose to build an INVINCIBLE brand, for all the right reasons. And choose to prevent the experience of an escalated crisis as a direct result.

Cheers to you and your organization!

REFERENCES

1. http://www.zappos.com/c/about-zappos

2. Quote: http://www.getelastic.com/good-customer-service-still-the-best-word-of-mouth-marketing-strategy/
    Story: http://www.huffingtonpost.com/great-work-cultures/real-business-is-about-pe_b_8484486.html

3. Zappos Company Culture Video: https://youtu.be/5CcLIPaUz3E

4. https://mountainviewpoliceblog.com/2014/05/14/an-open-letter-to-the-mountain-view-community-about-officers-arrest/

5. Quote taken from a recording of the police radio where Dan Linskey gave this order to his team. Recording provided to me by Dan.

6. *United Breaks Guitars* by Dave Carroll, and Wikipedia: https://en.wikipedia.org/wiki/United_Breaks_Guitars

7. http://www.journalnow.com/business/conover-domino-s-closes-in-wake-of-gross-out-video/article_12f0f5ee-7c53-55ba-9243-71add81df75a.html

8. https://en.wikipedia.org/wiki/United_Express_Flight_3411_incident and https://www.nytimes.com/2017/04/11/business/united-airline-passenger-overbooked-flights.html?_r=0

9. http://fortune.com/2017/04/11/united-airlines-stock-drop/

10. https://en.oxforddictionaries.com/definition/viral

11. https://www.theguardian.com/world/2015/jan/09/boko-haram-deadliest-massacre-baga-nigeria

12. http://money.cnn.com/2015/01/09/technology/social/jesuischarlie-hashtag-twitter/index.html, and https://en.wikipedia.org/wiki/Je_suis_Charlie#cite_note-twitter-7

13. https://en.wikipedia.org/wiki/Charlie_Hebdo_shooting#Reactions

14. http://www.huffingtonpost.com/2015/01/07/je-suis-charlie-creator_n_6432712.html

15. https://www.nytimes.com/2015/02/15/magazine/how-one-stupid-tweet-ruined-justine-saccos-life.html

16. http://pagesix.com/2014/08/04/hotel-charges-500-for-every-bad-review-posted-online/?utm_campaign=SocialFlow&utm_source=P6Twitter&utm_medium=SocialFlow

17. Video references: melissaagnes.com/emory, and https://youtu.be/63cTXQxntbw and https://youtu.be/T50gyPDa5sM

18. http://advancingyourhealth.org/highlights/posting-policy/faqs-about-the-ebola-virus-and-emory-university-hospital/#q1

19. http://advancingyourhealth.org/highlights/2014/08/01/emory-healthcare-ebola-patient/, and http://advancingyourhealth.org/highlights/2014/08/02/ebola-faq/

20. https://www.washingtonpost.com/posteverything/wp/2014/08/06/ im-the-head-nurse-at-emory-this-is-why-we-wanted-to-bring-the-ebola-patients-to-the-u-s/?utm_term=.40f24fc3926f

21. http://news.bbc.co.uk/1/hi/entertainment/4769730.stm, and https://en.wikipedia.org/wiki/Academy_Awards#cite_note-31

22. http://fortune.com/2017/03/02/oscars-2017-pwc-accountants-security/

23. https://www.nytimes.com/2017/01/11/business/volkswagen-diesel-vw-settlement-charges-criminal.html?_r=1, and https://en.wikipedia.org/wiki/Volkswagen_emissions_scandal

24. https://youtu.be/s-gvs2Y2368

25. http://www.nytimes.com/2009/04/16/business/media/16dominos. html

26. https://www.nytimes.com/2016/09/28/business/dealbook/wells-fargo-john-stumpf-compensation.html

27. http://money.cnn.com/2017/03/20/investing/wells-fargo-fake-accounts-credit-cards/index.html?iid=EL

28. http://money.cnn.com/2016/10/24/investing/wells-fargo-fake-accounts-angry-customers/index.html?iid=EL

29. http://time.com/4526350/samsung-galaxy-note-7-recall-problems-overheating-fire/

30. https://www.wsj.com/articles/bp-agrees-to-pay-18-7-billion-to-
     settle-deepwater-horizon-oil-spill-claims-1435842739?mg=prod/
     accounts-wsj, and
     https://www.wsj.com/articles/u-s-says-20-8-billion-bp-spill-
     settlement-finalized-1444058619

31. https://www.cnbc.com/2017/08/16/marcus-lemonis-if-youre-ok-
     with-what-trump-said-dont-shop-at-my-business.html

32. http://www.miami.com/miami-news/the-profit-star-marcus-
     lemonis-releases-statement-after-trump-comments-170111/

33. http://cincinnatizoo.org/blog/2016/05/28/media-update-gorilla-
     world/, and
     http://cincinnatizoo.org/blog/2016/05/29/cincinnati-zoo-
     devastated-by-death-of-beloved-gorilla/

34. https://apnews.com/30e2268f9c084dcfbee37ee7b716a362/harambe-
     lives-killed-zoo-gorilla-gets-second-life-online

35. http://www.bbc.co.uk/blogs/collegeofjournalism/entries/0f944ab7-
     9f96-4091-a927-db826630d997

ACKNOWLEDGMENTS

Sitting down to acknowledge everyone who has helped me bring this book into the world was both exciting and nerve-wracking—exciting because I'm so very grateful to the incredible and inspiring humans that I'm blessed to call friends, and nerve-wracking for the risk of leaving someone out. Since mitigating risk and turning it into opportunity is kind of my thing, let me suggest this: if I owe you an acknowledgement and I have somehow not included you here, I now also owe you champagne and look forward to you reaching out and giving me the pleasure of toasting you in person!

Having averted that potential crisis, I need to begin by thanking my partners in crime, Naren Aryal and the entire Mascot Books team. You all put up with my crazy meticulousness, and never once made me feel as though I was being a nuisance, even though I'm sure I was on at least a couple of occasions! Naren, your care and dedication to this project made me feel as though I was never in it alone—and the fun and jokes we've shared along the way have been an added perk! To my editor, Christopher Simon, thank you for your talent in helping me keep my message succinct, well-written, and unapologetic. Kristin Perry, thank you for all the work you put into keeping this project on track and organized, and for your dedicated attention to detail. Ricky Frame, you made this book beautiful, and you did it with such strategic thought and fervor; thank you!

To my speaker agent, Michelle Joyce, thank you for being my sounding board and for all the work you put into helping me crystalize my positioning. I'm so excited for all that's to come in our work together! Jamie Filotei, you are always there to encourage me and provide feedback; I really appreciate you.

Clint Greenleaf, you asked smart questions that helped me realize my approach to getting published was all wrong. As a result of your time, thoughtfulness, and introductions, I got to work with Mascot Books. Thank you.

Tim Vandehey, thank you for your brilliance in helping me develop the CRP concept and the Crisis Ready Rules!

Nick Morgan, thank you for your help in shaping this book in its early days, your persistence in the quest for getting it published, and all your continued guidance and support.

A huge thank you to the incredibly talented Neen James, who was able to take the complexity of my work and package it in such an easily comprehensible way. The Crisis Ready Model wouldn't exist without you, and watching you work your magic was astonishing! To Elise Eskanazi, the talent behind taking my pen-drawn Crisis Ready Model and making it strong yet quietly sophisticated...how you managed to make a triangle sexy, I'll never know, but I am extremely grateful!

To my person, Phil M. Jones, thank you for always being there to challenge me, and for understanding me the way you do. Your talent with words led to the outstanding headings and chapter titles found throughout these pages, and your ability to really hear what I wanted to achieve with the cover led to the perfect design on the face of this book.

To my beautiful friends back home, Jean-Michel Ghoussoub (a.k.a. Mr. Fabulous), Marylène Ayotte, Sacha Declomesnil, Sandra Gazel, and Sylvain Robillard, you all are such monstrous supports to me and I'm so blessed to have you in my life. Thank you for your unwavering friendship.

Last, and certainly not least, to Colt. To you, I dedicate this book. The book that you envisioned and believed in long before I was ready to. Your love, encouragement, and belief in me helped me find the confidence to share this important message. To you, I am eternally grateful.

ABOUT THE AUTHOR

It's awkward having to write about yourself. The good news (for me) is that, if you've already read the jacket of this book, the introduction, and the interlude, you already know a bunch about me and my career, which means I don't need to ramble on about it here.

I will say that I am grateful to have been able to build a career doing the thing that I am extremely passionate about: helping organizations build stronger, more invincible brands for the right reasons. This journey allows me the opportunity to advise some really great organizations and leaders, as different from one another as they are complex in their own right. From government to technology to healthcare and beyond, I have seen firsthand how crises unfold and have been in the position to ensure they are conquered, no matter the entity they strike.

As much as I would like to, the reality is that I can't work with every organization. This is where the pleasure and excitement in writing this book stemmed from—the fact that I got to lay it all out and share my entire framework and approach. If you've made it all the way to this page, then I'm going to choose to believe it's because you've read the pages that precede this one, in which case, I'd love to connect with you and learn about your experience in taking what you've learned throughout this book, and using it to implement a crisis ready culture within your organization.

If you're interested in connecting, feel free to email me at: melissa@melissaagnes.com

You can also connect with me on LinkedIn: linkedin.com/in/melissaagnes/

I can't wait to continue the conversation!

FURTHER WAYS TO BUILD BRAND INVINCIBILITY

What I care about most is helping your organization and team build an invincible brand by becoming truly crisis ready. With that in mind, following are some additional offerings that were designed to help you achieve your crisis ready objectives.

PUT *CRISIS READY* IN THE HANDS OF YOUR ENTIRE TEAM

Becoming crisis ready is cultural. Culture starts at the top and runs through the entirety of the organization from there. This book was designed with that in mind, and was written for your entire team—and I want to make it easy for you to get it into their hands.

If you're interested in ordering multiple copies of this book for your team, reach out to Mascot Books, at info@mascotbooks.com, and let's work together to get you the number of copies you need in an investment that makes sense for your organization.

CRISIS READY IS A KEYNOTE PRESENTATION TAILORED FOR YOUR TEAM

Crisis Ready is a keynote presentation and half-day workshop that I have delivered to dozens of organizations around the world. If you're interested in bringing this message to your team in a tailored way that will help you achieve some core internal objectives, then I'd love to have that conversation with you. Reach out to Michelle Joyce, at michelle@melissaagnes.com, and let's get started.

You can also visit melissaagnes.com for more information on the types of keynotes and workshops I deliver.